soufflé

soufflé

Sara Lewis

hamlyn

Notes

The Department of Health advises that eggs should not be consumed raw. This book contains some dishes made with raw or lightly cooked eggs. It is prudent for more vulnerable people such as pregnant and nursing mothers, invalids, the elderly, babies, and young children to avoid uncooked or lightly cooked dishes made with eggs.

Both metric and imperial measurements have been given.
Use one set of measurements only, and not a mixture of both.

Standard level spoon measurements are used in all recipes.
1 tablespoon = one 15 ml spoon
1 teaspoon = one 5 ml spoon

Full-fat milk should be used unless otherwise stated.
Fresh herbs should be used unless otherwise stated.
Large eggs should be used unless otherwise stated.

Ovens should be preheated to the specified temperature – if using a fan-assisted oven, follow the manufacturer's instructions for adjusting the time and the temperature.

First published in Great Britain in 2005 by
Hamlyn, a division of Octopus Publishing Group Ltd
2–4 Heron Quays, London E14 4JP

ISBN 0 600 61342 9
EAN 9780600613428

A CIP catalogue record for this book is available from the British Library

Printed and bound in China

10 9 8 7 6 5 4 3 2 1

contents

introduction

Soufflés may be baked and served straight from the oven, or uncooked and served chilled; they may also be sweet or savoury. The one thing all soufflés have in common is a light, airy texture due to the inclusion of whisked egg whites.

The classic soufflé is the hot, baked version, which was originally developed in France as a means of using up leftover food (creatively combined with the household staples of eggs and flour). In cookery terms, this is the soufflé regarded with the greatest respect and the one that most people shy away from making. They eat them only when they order one in a restaurant, and watch, transfixed, when a television chef pulls a perfectly risen creation from the oven, smiling triumphantly and ignoring the 15 previous takes that didn't quite go according to plan! The baked soufflé's tricky reputation derives from the fact that it relies on hot air to rise and so has a tendency to collapse as soon as it is removed from the oven.

This book will shatter the illusion of the impossible hot soufflé and show you that it's not actually that difficult to make one. All it takes is the right ingredients, the right techniques and a little dash of confidence.

'The only thing that will make a soufflé fall is if it knows you are afraid of it.'
James Beard

hot soufflés

A basic hot soufflé mixture consists of a thick base sauce (usually a roux-based white sauce for a savoury soufflé or a crème pâtissière for a sweet one) mixed with whisked egg whites, to which can be added almost any savoury or sweet flavouring – from cheese or chorizo to chocolate or fruit. The variations really are endless, as you'll discover from the recipes in this book.

Beat cheese into a hot, thick, roux-based white sauce with mustard and salt and pepper and stir until the cheese has melted.

Off the heat, stir the egg yolks into the flavoured sauce and beat until smooth.

Fold a large spoonful of whisked egg whites into the thick, cooled sauce to loosen the mixture, then gently fold in the remainder.

Gradually add dissolved gelatine in a thin, steady trickle to thickly whisked egg yolks and sugar.

Fold in flavourings such as puréed fruits or melted chocolate and softly whipped double cream.

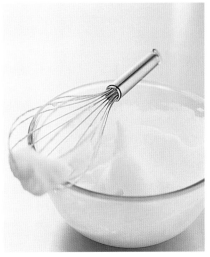

Whisk egg whites into stiff peaks, then fold a large spoonful into the cream mixture to loosen it, then gently fold in the remainder.

The mixture is spooned into a prepared soufflé dish and placed in a preheated oven. The trapped air in the whisked egg whites causes the soufflé to rise as it cooks. This accounts for its name, which loosely translates from the French *souffler* meaning 'to blow up'. At the end of the cooking time, a successful soufflé should emerge from the oven towering impressively above the rim of its mould, supported by a collar of paper tied around the dish with string. The soufflé is then served at once, still hot and wobbling, before it collapses.

chilled soufflés

These soufflés are mousse-like, sweet soufflés made with stiffly whisked, *uncooked* egg whites. This fact means that it is unwise to serve chilled soufflés to pregnant and nursing mothers, young children and the elderly.

They usually include thick cream and gelatine among the ingredients and require chilling (or freezing) in order to set. A chilled soufflé also relies on a paper collar around the dish. This allows the mixture to set proud of its mould and is removed on serving to produce a striking dessert.

tips for successful soufflés

Measure out all your ingredients before you begin. This is good practice when following any recipe so you won't forget any of the ingredients or discover you're missing something halfway through.

● Line the dish for a hot soufflé with ingredients such as flour or breadcrumbs (see page 8) to help the mixture rise as it cooks and prevent it from sticking to the sides of the mould. (The dish for a chilled soufflé does not need lining.)

● Make a paper collar (see page 8) for the soufflé dish to support the soufflé as it rises or sets.

● As with other recipes that use beaten egg whites – such as meringue – make sure your mixing bowl and whisk are clean and dry. If the bowl has been in the cupboard for a while, a quick wipe over is not sufficient: you'll need to wash and dry it carefully before use.

● For best results, chill your eggs in the refrigerator and separate them when they're still cold. However, allow the whites to come to room temperature before whisking them, as this will help to increase the volume of your soufflé by incorporating more air.

- Don't over-whisk the egg whites; they will become dry and it will be difficult to combine them with other ingredients.
- Use a plastic spatula when combining soufflé ingredients, and fold in the mixture as gently as possible.
- For soufflés that include gelatine in the ingredients, it's important to add this in a steady, continuous stream.
- Make sure the oven has reached the required temperature before you start to cook your soufflé. Place it in the centre of the oven to cook and don't open the oven door to check on progress during cooking until almost at the end, as the temperature will drop and your soufflé might be a flop.
- Some hot soufflés can be prepared in advance and then chilled until the stiffly whisked egg whites are added just before baking. This is useful if you're preparing a hot soufflé for a dinner party, as you'll have only the final cooking to do at the last minute.

Lining a soufflé dish

1 To line a dish in preparation for a hot soufflé, grease the base and sides of the dish with butter and then sprinkle in a tablespoon of sugar or ground almonds (for sweet soufflés) or flour, breadcrumbs, ground nuts or grated cheese (for savoury soufflés).

2 Tilt the dish and tap it gently, turning it around, so that your chosen ingredient covers the inside of the dish evenly.

3 Tip out any excess sugar, flour or other ingredient being used for the lining.

Making a soufflé collar

1 To make a collar for a soufflé, cut a length of baking parchment (also known as parchment paper) slightly longer than the circumference of the soufflé dish. Fold it in half lengthways so that it will be strong enough to support the soufflé.

2 Wrap the length of paper around the outside of the dish so that it stands higher than the top of the dish – no more than 7.5 cm (3 in). Fix in place with a length of string and knot tightly.

3 Just before serving, snip the string and carefully remove the paper collar.

Spread butter or olive oil over the base and sides of an ovenproof soufflé dish.

For a savoury soufflé, sprinkle the base and sides of the dish with flour or breadcrumbs, finely grated cheese or ground nuts.

For a sweet soufflé, sprinkle the base and sides of the dish with caster sugar, ground nuts or flour, tilting the dish for even coverage.

Wrap a folded length of baking parchment around the dish so that the ends overlap and the paper stands 4–7.5 cm (1½–3in) high.

Tie the paper securely in place with fine string and snip off the ends.

When the soufflé has set (or cooked), snip off the string and peel away the paper, using a knife to prevent the soufflé edge from tearing.

equipment

Soufflés are not complicated dishes to cook, and therefore the list of necessary equipment is not long.

• **Soufflé dish** The most important thing to consider for hot soufflés is the actual soufflé dish. The ideal shape is cylindrical with straight, smooth sides so that the soufflé can rise easily and will not catch on the sides or between ridges. Soufflé dishes are ideally made of ovenproof porcelain, but whatever dish you use, it should be suitably heatproof. Depending on the recipe, you may require one large dish or a number of smaller dishes (known as ramekins) for individual servings. If you don't have a specific soufflé dish, soufflés can, in theory, be cooked in any straight-sided heatproof container – the important thing is to ensure that you use the correct size for the mixture. Five different sizes of soufflé dishes have been used for the recipes in this book, ranging from 7.5 cm (3 in) diameter x 4 cm (1½ in) deep individual soufflé dishes to a medium tall 15 cm (6 in) diameter x 9 cm (3¾ in) deep dish.

• **Mixing bowl** Use a stainless steel or glass mixing bowl when whisking the eggs. It is easier to get these bowls absolutely clean – plastic can sometimes retain oil on its surface, which will prevent your egg whites from stiffening.

• **Whisk** You could use a hand whisk for whisking the eggs, but an electric one will save you time and energy.

• **Additional items** You will also need baking parchment, a pair of scissors and some string for soufflé collars, and oven gloves are essential for transferring a hot soufflé from the oven to the table as quickly as possible.

start souffléing!

Now that you know all there is to know about making soufflés, choose a recipe from among the following pages, buy the ingredients and put a soufflé on the menu tonight. Try Black Olive and Basil Soufflés served with roasted tomatoes (page 17) for a light meal, Twice-Baked Cheese and Walnut Soufflés (page 24) for a special occasion, or how about the decadent White Choc Soufflés with Dark Chocolate Sauce (page 32) to indulge a sweet tooth? Once you've perfected the art of making soufflés, you could find yourself rustling one up every other day, whether for lunch or dinner!

hot savoury
soufflés

triple-cheese soufflé with apple compote

65 g (2¹/2 oz) butter

50 g (2 oz) Parmesan cheese, freshly
    grated

50 g (2 oz) strong Cheddar cheese,
    grated

75 g (3 oz) Gruyère cheese, rind
    removed, grated

50 g (2 oz) plain flour

300 ml (1/2 pint) milk

1 teaspoon Dijon mustard

4 eggs, separated

large pinch of cayenne pepper

salt

green salad, to serve

Apple compote

15 g (1/2 oz) butter

2 dessert apples, cored and thickly
    sliced

1 tablespoon caster sugar

1 tablespoon cider vinegar

4 tablespoons water

Serves 4

Preparation time: 30 minutes

Cooking time: 30–35 minutes

This rich, soft cheese soufflé contrasts well with the tangy sharpness of the warm apple compote to make a luxurious light lunch or supper dish. You could experiment if you like and make up your own triple-cheese combinations.

1 Grease a medium tall 15 cm (6 in) diameter x 9 cm (3³/4 in) deep soufflé dish with some of the butter. Mix the three cheeses together, then use 3 tablespoons to line the dish (see page 8). Attach a soufflé collar that stands 7.5 cm (3 in) higher than the top of the dish (see page 8).

2 Melt the remaining butter in a saucepan, stir in the flour and cook for 1 minute. Gradually mix in the milk and bring to the boil, stirring until thickened and smooth.

3 Stir in the remaining cheeses, mustard, egg yolks, cayenne pepper and a little salt. Cover and leave to cool.

4 Whisk the egg whites into stiff, moist-looking peaks. Fold a large spoonful into the cooled sauce to loosen the mixture, then fold in the remaining egg whites.

5 Pour the mixture into the prepared soufflé dish and bake in a preheated oven, 190°C (375°F), Gas Mark 5, for 25–30 minutes until the soufflé is well risen, the top is browned and there is a slight wobble to the centre.

6 While the soufflé cooks, melt the butter for the compote in a small frying pan, add the apples and fry for 4–5 minutes until hot. Sprinkle with the sugar, cook for 2–3 minutes until just beginning to brown then add the vinegar and water and simmer for 2–3 minutes until syrupy.

7 Quickly snip the string off the soufflé collar and gently peel away the paper. Spoon the soufflé on to plates. Serve with the apple compote and a green salad.

smoked salmon and dill soufflé

65 g (2¹/2 oz) butter
3 tablespoons fresh breadcrumbs
50 g (2 oz) plain flour
300 ml (¹/2 pint) milk
4 tablespoons full-fat crème fraîche
3 tablespoons chopped dill
grated rind of 1 lemon
4 eggs, separated
100 g (3¹/2 oz) sliced smoked salmon,
    cut into thin strips
salt and freshly ground black pepper

To serve
slices of smoked salmon (optional)
lemon wedges

Serves 4
Preparation time: 30 minutes
Cooking time: 35–40 minutes

1 Grease a medium tall 15 cm (6 in) diameter x 9 cm (3³/4 in) deep soufflé dish with some of the butter, then line the dish with the breadcrumbs (see page 8). Attach a soufflé collar that stands 7.5 cm (3 in) higher than the top of the dish (see page 8).

2 Melt the remaining butter in a saucepan, stir in the flour and cook for 1 minute. Gradually mix in the milk and bring to the boil, stirring until thickened and smooth.

3 Remove the pan from the heat and stir in the crème fraîche, dill, lemon rind, egg yolks and some salt and pepper. Cover and leave to cool.

4 Whisk the egg whites into stiff, moist-looking peaks. Fold the strips of smoked salmon into the cooled sauce, then a large spoonful of egg whites to loosen the mixture. Gently fold in the remaining egg whites.

5 Pour the mixture into the prepared soufflé dish so that it is three-quarters full. Bake in a preheated oven, 190°C (375°F), Gas Mark 5, for 30–35 minutes until the soufflé is well risen, the top is browned and there is a slight wobble to the centre.

6 Quickly snip the string off the soufflé collar and gently peel away the paper. Spoon the soufflé on to plates. Serve with extra slices of smoked salmon, if using, and lemon wedges.

roasted pepper and rosemary soufflé

1 red pepper, cored, deseeded and cut
    into 8 pieces
1 orange pepper, cored, deseeded and
    cut into 8 pieces
2 garlic cloves, finely chopped
2 tablespoons olive oil
1 tablespoon balsamic vinegar
65 g (2¹/2 oz) butter
2 tablespoons ready-grated Parmesan
    cheese
50 g (2 oz) plain flour
300 ml (1/2 pint) milk
2 tablespoons chopped rosemary
125 g (4 oz) provolone, Gruyère or
    strong Cheddar cheese, grated
4 eggs, separated
salt and freshly ground black pepper
dressed rocket salad, to serve

Serves 4
Preparation time: 30 minutes
Cooking time: 38–45 minutes

Packed with colourful strips of roasted red and orange pepper and flavoured with rosemary and garlic, this Mediterranean-inspired soufflé makes a great weekend lunch dish to follow a bowl of steaming soup in winter or a light summer salad.

1 Put the pieces of pepper, skin side uppermost, in the base of a grill pan, sprinkle with the chopped garlic and drizzle with the oil. Grill for 8–10 minutes until the skins are blackened and the peppers softened. Turn the peppers over, then drizzle with the vinegar, cover with foil and leave to cool.

2 Meanwhile, grease a medium tall 15 cm (6 in) diameter x 9 cm (3³/4 in) deep soufflé dish with some of the butter, then line the dish with the Parmesan (see page 8). Attach a soufflé collar that stands 7.5 cm (3 in) higher than the top of the dish (see page 8).

3 Melt the remaining butter in a saucepan, stir in the flour and cook for 1 minute. Gradually mix in the milk and bring to the boil, stirring until thickened and smooth.

4 Remove the pan from the heat and stir in the rosemary and grated cheese. Beat in the egg yolks and some salt and pepper. Cover and leave to cool.

5 Peel the skins off the peppers using a small, sharp knife, thinly slice the flesh then stir into the cooled sauce. Whisk the egg whites into stiff, moist-looking peaks. Fold a large spoonful into the pepper mixture to loosen it, then gently fold in the remaining egg whites.

6 Spoon the mixture into the prepared soufflé dish and bake in a preheated oven, 190°C (375°F), Gas Mark 5, for 25–30 minutes until the soufflé is well risen, the top is browned and there is a slight wobble to the centre.

7 Quickly snip the string off the soufflé collar and gently peel away the paper. Spoon the soufflé on to plates. Serve with a dressed rocket salad.

stilton soufflé with rocket

65 g (2 1/2 oz) butter
3 tablespoons fresh breadcrumbs
50 g (2 oz) plain flour
300 ml (1/2 pint) milk
150 g (5 oz) Stilton cheese, rind
   removed, cheese crumbled
4 eggs, separated
25 g (1 oz) wild rocket leaves, torn into
   pieces, plus extra to serve
salt and freshly ground black pepper
balsamic vinegar, to serve

Serves 4
Preparation time: 30 minutes
Cooking time: 35–40 minutes

Creamy blue cheese complements the peppery taste of rocket beautifully in this tasty soufflé. Watercress or sorrel could be used instead of the rocket leaves.

1 Grease a medium tall 15 cm (6 in) diameter x 9 cm (3 3/4 in) deep soufflé dish with some of the butter, then line the dish with the breadcrumbs (see page 8). Attach a soufflé collar that stands 7.5 cm (3 in) higher than the top of the dish (see page 8).

2 Melt the remaining butter in a saucepan, stir in the flour and cook for 1 minute. Gradually mix in the milk and bring to the boil, stirring until thickened and smooth.

3 Stir in the cheese until melted, then remove from the heat and stir in the egg yolks and some salt and pepper. Cover and leave to cool.

4 Whisk the egg whites into stiff, moist-looking peaks. Fold the rocket leaves into the cooled sauce, then a large spoonful of egg whites to loosen the mixture. Gently fold in the remaining egg whites.

5 Pour the mixture into the prepared soufflé dish and bake in a preheated oven, 190°C (375°F), Gas Mark 5, for 30–35 minutes until the soufflé is well risen, the top is browned and there is a slight wobble to the centre.

6 Quickly snip the string off the soufflé collar and gently peel away the paper. Spoon the soufflé on to plates. Serve with extra rocket leaves dressed with balsamic vinegar.

black olive and basil soufflés

65 g (2¹/2 oz) butter
75 g (3 oz) Parmesan cheese, freshly
    grated
50 g (2 oz) plain flour
300 ml (1/2 pint) milk
4 eggs, separated
50 g (2 oz) pitted black olives, sliced
4 tablespoons chopped basil
salt and freshly ground black pepper
roasted cherry tomatoes, to serve

Serves 4
Preparation time: 30 minutes
Cooking time: 25–30 minutes

1 Grease 4 small 10 cm (4 in) diameter x 6 cm (2¹/2 in) deep soufflé dishes with some of the butter, then line the dishes with 3 tablespoons of the Parmesan (see page 8).

2 Melt the remaining butter in a saucepan, stir in the flour and cook for 1 minute. Gradually mix in the milk and bring to the boil, stirring until thickened and smooth.

3 Remove the pan from the heat and stir in the remaining Parmesan and the egg yolks, then the olives and some salt and pepper. Cover and leave to cool.

4 Whisk the egg whites into stiff, moist-looking peaks. Fold a large spoonful into the cooled sauce, along with the chopped basil, to loosen the mixture, then gently fold in the remaining egg whites.

5 Pour the mixture into the prepared soufflé dishes and bake in a preheated oven, 190°C (375°F), Gas Mark 5, for 15–20 minutes until the soufflés are well risen, the tops are browned and there is a slight wobble to the centres. Serve immediately with roasted cherry tomatoes.

spinach and pine nut soufflés

65 g (2¹/2 oz) butter

3 tablespoons ready-grated Parmesan
   cheese

300 g (10 oz) frozen leaf spinach,
   defrosted

50 g (2 oz) plain flour

300 ml (¹/2 pint) milk

100 g (3¹/2 oz) cream cheese

1 garlic clove, finely crushed

large pinch of grated nutmeg

4 egg yolks

40 g (1¹/2 oz) pine nuts

5 egg whites

salt and freshly ground black pepper

Serves 4
Preparation time: 30 minutes
Cooking time: 25 minutes

Forget about tedious rinsing and picking over of spinach leaves, this vibrant green-speckled soufflé is made with labour-saving frozen spinach and flavoured with pine nuts and just a hint of garlic and nutmeg.

1 Grease 4 small 10 cm (4 in) diameter x 6 cm (2¹/2 in) deep soufflé dishes with some of the butter, then line the dishes with the Parmesan (see page 8). Attach a soufflé collar to each dish that stands 6 cm (2¹/2 in) higher than the top of the dish (see page 8). Stand the dishes on a baking sheet. Put the spinach in a sieve set over a bowl and press out any water using the back of a spoon.

2 Melt the remaining butter in a saucepan, stir in the flour and cook for 1 minute. Gradually mix in the milk and bring to the boil, stirring until thickened and smooth.

3 Remove the pan from the heat and stir in the cream cheese, garlic and nutmeg. Mix in the egg yolks, spinach, half the pine nuts and some salt and pepper. Cover and leave to cool.

4 Whisk the egg whites into stiff, moist-looking peaks. Fold a large spoonful of the whites into the cooled sauce to loosen the mixture, then gently fold in the remaining egg whites.

5 Spoon the mixture into the prepared soufflé dishes, then sprinkle with the remaining pine nuts. Bake in a preheated oven, 190°C (375°F), Gas Mark 5, for 20 minutes until the soufflés are well risen, their tops are browned and there is a slight wobble to the centres. Quickly snip the string off the soufflé collar and gently peel away the paper. Serve immediately.

roasted onion and soured cream soufflé

75 g (3 oz) butter
1 tablespoon olive oil
250 g (8 oz) large onions, thinly sliced
1 teaspoon caster sugar
3 tablespoons ready-grated Parmesan
    cheese
50 g (2 oz) plain flour
200 ml (7 fl oz) milk
150 ml (1/4 pint) soured cream
75 g (3 oz) Gruyère cheese, grated
a little grated nutmeg
4 eggs, separated
salt and freshly ground black pepper

To serve
green salad
crusty bread

Serves 4
Preparation time: 30 minutes
Cooking time: 40–45 minutes

Long, slow cooking of the onions results in a mellow, naturally sweeter flavour, which is heightened with just a sprinkling of sugar to caramelize them. Mixed with the smoothness of soured cream and the nuttiness of grated Gruyère, it makes a delicious combination.

1 Heat 15 g ($^1/_2$ oz) of the butter and the oil in a frying pan. Add the onions and fry gently for 10 minutes, stirring occasionally, until softened and just beginning to turn golden. Sprinkle with the sugar and cook for 5 more minutes until lightly caramelized.

2 Meanwhile, grease a medium tall 15 cm (6 in) diameter x 9 cm ($3^3/_4$ in) deep soufflé dish with some of the remaining butter, then line the dish with the Parmesan (see page 8). Attach a soufflé collar that stands 7.5 cm (3 in) higher than the top of the dish (see page 8).

3 Melt the remaining butter in a saucepan, stir in the flour and cook for 1 minute. Gradually mix in the milk and bring to the boil, stirring until thickened and smooth.

4 Remove the pan from the heat and stir in the soured cream, then the Gruyère and nutmeg. Beat in the egg yolks and some salt and pepper. Cover and leave to cool.

5 Whisk the egg whites into stiff, moist-looking peaks. Fold the cooked onions into the cooled sauce, then a large spoonful of egg whites to loosen the mixture. Gently fold in the remaining egg whites.

6 Pour the mixture into the prepared soufflé dish and bake in a preheated oven, 190°C (375°F), Gas Mark 5, for 25–30 minutes until the soufflé is well risen, the top is browned and there is a slight wobble to the centre.

7 Quickly snip the string off the soufflé collar and gently peel away the paper. Spoon the soufflé on to plates. Serve with a green salad and crusty bread.

garlic mushroom soufflé

Serve this delicious, craggy-topped soufflé for a leisurely Sunday brunch accompanied by crispy bacon rashers and griddled tomatoes. If you have trouble finding mixed packs of 'exotic' mushrooms, then use button or chestnut mushrooms on their own.

65 g (2¹/2 oz) butter
3 tablespoons ready-grated Parmesan
    cheese
2 tablespoons olive oil
150 g (5 oz) mixed mushrooms, to
    include baby chestnut, shiitake
    and oyster, sliced
2 garlic cloves, crushed
50 g (2 oz) plain flour
300 ml (1/2 pint) milk
1 teaspoon wholegrain mustard
4 eggs, separated
salt and freshly ground black pepper

To serve
crispy bacon
griddled tomatoes

Serves 4
Preparation time: 30 minutes
Cooking time: 33–38 minutes

1 Grease a medium tall 15 cm (6 in) diameter x 9 cm (3³/4 in) deep soufflé dish with some of the butter, then line the dish with the Parmesan (see page 8). Attach a soufflé collar that stands 7.5 cm (3 in) higher than the top of the dish (see page 8).

2 Heat the oil in a frying pan. Add the chestnut and shiitake mushrooms and garlic and fry for 2 minutes, stirring, then add the oyster mushrooms and cook for 1 minute. Leave to cool.

3 Melt the remaining butter in a saucepan, stir in the flour and cook for 1 minute. Gradually mix in the milk and bring to the boil, stirring until thickened and smooth. Stir in the mustard, egg yolks and some salt and pepper. Cover and leave to cool.

4 Whisk the egg whites into stiff, moist-looking peaks. Fold a large spoonful of egg whites into the cooled sauce to loosen the mixture, then fold in the cooked mushrooms. Gently fold in the remaining egg whites.

5 Pour the mixture into the prepared soufflé dish and bake in a preheated oven, 190°C (375°F), Gas Mark 5, for 25–30 minutes until the soufflé is well risen, the top is browned and there is a slight wobble to the centre.

6 Quickly snip the string off the soufflé collar and gently peel away the paper. Spoon the soufflé on to plates. Serve with crispy bacon and griddled tomatoes.

fine herb, ricotta and shallot soufflé

65 g (2¹/2 oz) butter
3 tablespoons fresh breadcrumbs
1 tablespoon olive oil
125 g (4 oz) shallots, finely chopped
50 g (2 oz) plain flour
300 ml (¹/2 pint) milk
125 g (4 oz) ricotta cheese
4 egg yolks
5 egg whites
2 tablespoons chopped mixed herbs,
    to include rosemary, sage and thyme
4 tablespoons chopped parsley or
    chives
salt and freshly ground black pepper
roasted cherry tomatoes, to serve

Serves 4
Preparation time: 30 minutes
Cooking time: 35–40 minutes

1 Grease a medium tall 15 cm (6 in) diameter x 9 cm (3³/4 in) deep soufflé dish with some of the butter, then line the dish with the breadcrumbs (see page 8). Attach a soufflé collar that stands 7.5 cm (3 in) higher than the top of the dish (see page 8).

2 Heat the oil in a frying pan, add the shallots and fry gently for 5 minutes, stirring frequently, until softened and just beginning to turn golden.

3 Meanwhile, melt the remaining butter in a saucepan, stir in the flour and cook for 1 minute. Gradually mix in the milk and bring to the boil, stirring until thickened and smooth.

4 Remove the pan from the heat and stir in the ricotta cheese, egg yolks, cooked shallots and some salt and pepper. Cover and leave to cool.

5 Whisk the egg whites into stiff, moist-looking peaks. Add the chopped herbs to the cooled sauce, then fold in a large spoonful of egg whites to loosen the mixture. Gently fold in the remaining egg whites.

6 Pour the mixture into the prepared soufflé dish and bake in a preheated oven, 190°C (375°F), Gas Mark 5, for 25–30 minutes until the soufflé is well risen, the top is browned and there is a slight wobble to the centre.

7 Quickly snip the string off the soufflé collar and gently peel away the paper. Spoon the soufflé on to plates. Serve with roasted cherry tomatoes.

twice-baked cheese and walnut soufflés

Unlike other hot savoury soufflés, twice-baked ones have one fewer egg white so that they are easier to handle when turning out of their dishes. Make and bake them earlier in the day, then reheat them when required, bathed with double cream peppered with chopped tarragon and a sprinkling of Parmesan.

40 g (1¹/2 oz) butter, plus extra for greasing

40 g (1¹/2 oz) plain flour

250 ml (8 fl oz) milk

100 g (3¹/2 oz) individual goats' cheese, diced

40 g (1¹/2 oz) walnut pieces, roughly chopped

3 egg yolks

2 egg whites

salt and freshly ground black pepper

To finish

300 ml (1/2 pint) double cream

1 teaspoon Dijon mustard

3 teaspoons chopped tarragon

2 tablespoons freshly grated Parmesan cheese

salt and freshly ground black pepper

Serves 6

Preparation time: 30 minutes

Cooking time: 20 minutes

Reheating time: 12–15 minutes

1 Lightly butter 6 individual 7.5 cm (3 in) diameter x 4 cm (1¹/2 in) deep soufflé dishes, then stand them on a rack in a roasting tin.

2 Melt the butter in a saucepan, stir in the flour and cook for 1 minute. Gradually mix in the milk and bring to the boil, stirring until thickened and smooth.

3 Remove the pan from the heat and stir in the goats' cheese, beating until melted. Mix in the walnut pieces, egg yolks and some salt and pepper. Cover and leave to cool for 15 minutes.

4 Whisk the egg whites into stiff, moist-looking peaks. Fold a spoonful into the cooled sauce to loosen the mixture, then gently fold in the remaining egg whites. Divide the mixture between the prepared soufflé dishes.

5 Pour hot water into the roasting tin to come halfway up the sides of the dishes, then bake, uncovered, in a preheated oven, 180°C (350°F), Gas Mark 4, for 15 minutes until the soufflés are well risen and spongy to the touch. Lift the dishes out of the tin, cool slightly then run a knife around the edges and unmould the soufflés into a buttered shallow ovenproof dish, leaving a little room between them.

6 When ready to reheat, make the sauce by mixing together the cream, mustard, tarragon and some salt and pepper, then pour this sauce over and around the soufflés. Sprinkle with the Parmesan and bake in a preheated oven, 180°C (350°F), Gas Mark 4, for 12–15 minutes until golden and the soufflés have puffed up slightly. Serve immediately.

twice-baked pecorino soufflés

40 g (1 1/2 oz) butter, plus extra for
    greasing
40 g (1 1/2 oz) plain flour
250 ml (8 fl oz) milk
50 g (2 oz) freshly grated pecorino or
    Parmesan cheese
3 egg yolks
2 egg whites
salt and freshly ground black pepper

Tomato sauce
1 tablespoon olive oil
1 small onion, finely chopped
400 g (13 oz) cherry tomatoes,
    quartered
1 garlic clove, crushed
1 teaspoon caster sugar
4 tablespoons dry white wine
salt and freshly ground black pepper

To finish
2 tablespoons freshly grated pecorino
    or Parmesan cheese
tiny basil leaves, to garnish

Serves 6
Preparation time: 30 minutes
Cooking time: 15 minutes
Reheating time: 12–15 minutes

These Italian-inspired mini soufflés can be made completely in advance, then reheated with the cherry tomato sauce at the last minute to make a hot starter. If you are pressed for time, use a can of good quality chopped tomatoes instead of the fresh ones.

1 Lightly butter 6 individual 7.5 cm (3 in) diameter x 4 cm (1 1/2 in) deep soufflé dishes, then stand them on a rack in a roasting tin.

2 Melt the butter in a saucepan, stir in the flour and cook for 1 minute. Gradually mix in the milk and bring to the boil, stirring until thickened and smooth.

3 Remove the pan from the heat and stir in the cheese, beating until melted. Mix in the egg yolks and some salt and pepper. Cover and leave to cool for 15 minutes.

4 Whisk the egg whites into stiff, moist-looking peaks. Fold a spoonful into the cooled sauce to loosen the mixture, then gently fold in the remaining egg whites. Divide the mixture between the prepared soufflé dishes.

5 Pour hot water into the roasting tin to come halfway up the sides of the dishes, then bake, uncovered, in a preheated oven, 180°C (350°F), Gas Mark 4, for 15 minutes until the soufflés are well risen and spongy to the touch. Lift the dishes out of the tin, cool slightly then run a knife around the edges and unmould the soufflés into a buttered shallow ovenproof dish, leaving a little room between them.

6 Meanwhile, make the tomato sauce by heating the oil in a saucepan. Add the onion and fry for 5 minutes, stirring frequently, until softened. Add the tomatoes, garlic, sugar, wine and some salt and pepper. Simmer for 5 minutes until thickened.

7 When ready to reheat, spoon the tomato sauce over and around the soufflés. Sprinkle with the cheese and bake in a preheated oven, 180°C (350°F), Gas Mark 4, for 12–15 minutes until the soufflés are golden and have puffed up slightly. Serve immediately, garnished with tiny basil leaves.

fruits de mer soufflé

65 g (2¹/2 oz) butter

2 tablespoons ready-grated Parmesan
    cheese

50 g (2 oz) plain flour

300 ml (1/2 pint) milk

grated rind of 1 lemon

4 eggs, separated

250 g (8 oz) mixed seafood, defrosted if
    frozen, rinsed with cold water and
    very roughly chopped

4 tablespoons chopped chives

salt and freshly ground black pepper

To serve
watercress salad
crusty bread
lemon wedges

Serves 4
Preparation time: 30 minutes
Cooking time: 35–40 minutes

This gourmet-style seafood soufflé is packed with chunky pieces of prawn, mussel and squid and flavoured with chopped chives and lemon. It makes a delightful light supper dish served with a crisp watercress salad and warm crusty bread.

1 Grease a medium tall 15 cm (6 in) diameter x 9 cm (3³/4 in) deep soufflé dish with some of the butter, then line the dish with the Parmesan (see page 8). Attach a soufflé collar that stands 7.5 cm (3 in) higher than the top of the dish (see page 8).

2 Melt the remaining butter in a saucepan, stir in the flour and cook for 1 minute. Gradually mix in the milk and bring to the boil, stirring until thickened and smooth.

3 Remove the pan from the heat and stir in the lemon rind, egg yolks and some salt and pepper. Cover and leave to cool.

4 Whisk the egg whites into stiff, moist-looking peaks. Fold a large spoonful into the cooled sauce to loosen the mixture, then fold in the seafood and chives. Gently fold in the remaining egg whites.

5 Spoon the mixture into the prepared soufflé dish and bake in a preheated oven, 190°C (375°F), Gas Mark 5, for 30–35 minutes until the soufflé is well risen, the top is browned and there is a slight wobble to the centre.

6 Quickly snip the string off the soufflé collar and gently peel away the paper. Spoon the soufflé on to plates. Serve with a watercress salad, warm crusty bread and lemon wedges.

sautéed fennel and parma ham soufflés

65 g (2¹/2 oz) butter
3 tablespoons fresh breadcrumbs
200 g (7 oz) fennel bulb
1 tablespoon olive oil
50 g (2 oz) plain flour
300 ml (¹/2 pint) milk
4 eggs, separated
75 g (3 oz) sliced Parma ham, cut into
    pieces
salt and freshly ground black pepper

Serves 4
Preparation time: 30 minutes
Cooking time: 25–30 minutes

Fennel is one of those vegetables that is seldom used and yet its delicate aniseed flavour goes well with milky sauces or creamy dishes. It is generally sold trimmed, but if there are a lot of green feathery tops still in place, then chop these and use 2 tablespoons in the soufflé.

1   Grease 4 small 10 cm (4 in) diameter x 6 cm (2¹/2 in) deep soufflé dishes with some of the butter, then line the dishes with the breadcrumbs (see page 8). Stand the dishes on a baking sheet.

2   Halve the fennel, cut out the woody core and discard. Reserve any green feathery tops and finely chop the remaining fennel. Heat the oil in a frying pan, add the chopped fennel and fry gently for 5 minutes, stirring occasionally, until softened. Chop and add any green tops.

3   Meanwhile, melt the remaining butter in a saucepan, stir in the flour and cook for 1 minute. Gradually mix in the milk and bring to the boil, stirring until thickened and smooth.

4   Remove the pan from the heat and stir in the egg yolks, then the sautéed fennel and some salt and pepper. Cover and leave to cool.

5   Whisk the egg whites into stiff, moist-looking peaks. Fold a large spoonful into the cooled sauce to loosen the mixture, then fold in the pieces of Parma ham. Gently fold in the remaining egg whites.

6   Pour the mixture into the prepared soufflé dishes and bake in a preheated oven, 190°C (375°F), Gas Mark 5, for 15–20 minutes until the soufflés are well risen, their tops are browned and there is a slight wobble to the centres. Serve immediately.

hot peppered chorizo soufflés

65 g (2¹/₂ oz) butter
3 tablespoons fresh breadcrumbs
50 g (2 oz) plain flour
300 ml (¹/₂ pint) milk
100 g (3¹/₂ oz) manchego or Cheddar
　　cheese, grated
¹/₂–1 teaspoon ready-chopped red chilli
4 eggs, separated
50 g (2 oz) sliced chorizo sausage,
　　diced
salt and freshly ground black pepper
green salad, to serve

Serves 4
Preparation time: 30 minutes
Cooking time: 20–25 minutes

1 Grease 4 small 10 cm (4 in) diameter x 6 cm (2¹/₂ in) deep soufflé dishes with some of the butter, then line the dishes with the breadcrumbs (see page 8). Stand the dishes on a baking sheet.

2 Melt the remaining butter in a saucepan, stir in the flour and cook for 1 minute. Gradually mix in the milk and bring to the boil, stirring until thickened and smooth.

3 Remove the pan from the heat and stir in the cheese, chilli to taste, egg yolks and some salt and pepper. Cover and leave to cool.

4 Whisk the egg whites into stiff, moist-looking peaks. Fold the diced chorizo sausage into the cooled sauce, then a large spoonful of egg whites to loosen the mixture. Gently fold in the remaining egg whites.

5 Spoon the mixture into the prepared soufflé dishes and bake in a preheated oven, 190°C (375°F), Gas Mark 5, for 15–20 minutes until the soufflés are well risen, their tops are browned and there is a slight wobble to the centres. Serve immediately with a crisp green salad.

hot and chilled
sweet soufflés

butter, for greasing

75 g (3 oz) caster sugar, plus
   4 teaspoons for lining the dishes

3 egg yolks

40 g (1½ oz) plain flour

250 ml (8 fl oz) milk

175 g (6 oz) white chocolate,
   roughly chopped

1 teaspoon vanilla essence

5 egg whites

sifted drinking chocolate powder and
   icing sugar, for dusting

Chocolate sauce

150 g (5 oz) plain dark chocolate,
   broken into pieces

125 ml (4 fl oz) milk

4 tablespoons double cream

25 g (1 oz) caster sugar

Serves 4
Preparation time: 30 minutes
Cooking time: 15–20 minutes

For chocoholics, these light, fluffy soufflés will prove to be a winner! Dotted with just-melted chunks of white chocolate, they are served with a glossy, rich, velvety, dark chocolate sauce enriched with double cream.

1 Lightly butter 4 small 10 cm (4 in) diameter x 6 cm (2½ in) deep soufflé dishes, then line each dish with 1 teaspoon caster sugar (see page 8). Stand the dishes on a baking sheet.

2 Whisk half the remaining caster sugar and the egg yolks in a bowl until thick, pale and mousse-like. Sift the flour over the surface, then gently fold it in.

3 Bring the milk just to the boil in a saucepan, then gradually whisk it into the egg yolk mixture. Return the milk mixture to the pan and cook over a medium heat, stirring continuously until thickened and smooth. Remove the pan from the heat, add half the white chocolate and stir until melted. Mix in the vanilla essence, cover and leave to cool.

4 Whisk the egg whites into stiff, moist-looking peaks. Gradually whisk in the remaining caster sugar, a teaspoon at a time, until thick and glossy. Fold a large spoonful of egg whites into the cooled sauce to loosen the mixture then fold in the remaining white chocolate. Gently fold in the remaining egg whites.

5 Spoon the mixture into the prepared soufflé dishes and bake in a preheated oven, 220°C (425°F), Gas Mark 7, for 10–12 minutes until the soufflés are well risen, their tops are browned and there is a slight wobble to the centres.

6 Meanwhile, gently heat all the sauce ingredients together in a small saucepan, stirring until smooth, then pour into a serving jug. Dust the tops of the soufflés with sifted drinking chocolate powder and icing sugar and serve immediately, with some of the warmed sauce drizzled over each one.

dark chocolate soufflé with crème anglaise

butter, for greasing
100 g (3½ oz) caster sugar, plus
   1 tablespoon for lining the dish
3 egg yolks
40 g (1½ oz) plain flour
250 ml (8 fl oz) milk
125 g (4 oz) plain dark chocolate,
   broken into pieces
5 egg whites
sifted drinking chocolate powder and
   icing sugar, for dusting

Crème anglaise
2 egg yolks
2 tablespoons caster sugar
1 teaspoon cornflour
250 ml (8 fl oz) milk
2 tablespoons double cream
½ teaspoon vanilla essence

Serves 4
Preparation time: 30 minutes
Cooking time: 30–35 minutes

This incredibly rich, bittersweet, dark chocolate soufflé is served with a creamy smooth vanilla custard sauce for an irresistible mealtime finale. You can make the soufflé base and crème anglaise earlier in the day if preferred, but sprinkle the surface of the custard with a little extra sugar or place a piece of wetted baking parchment on it to prevent a skin forming.

1 Lightly butter a medium tall 15 cm (6 in) diameter x 9 cm (3¾ in) deep soufflé dish, then line the dish with 1 tablespoon caster sugar (see page 8). Attach a soufflé collar that stands 7.5 cm (3 in) higher than the top of the dish (see page 8).

2 Whisk half the remaining caster sugar and the egg yolks in a bowl until thick, pale and mousse-like. Sift the flour over the surface, then gently fold it in.

3 Bring the milk just to the boil in a saucepan, then gradually whisk it into the egg yolk mixture. Return the milk mixture to the pan and cook over a medium heat, stirring continuously until thickened and smooth. Remove from the heat, add the chocolate and stir until melted. Cover and leave to cool.

4 Whisk the egg whites into stiff, moist-looking peaks. Gradually whisk in the remaining caster sugar, a teaspoon at a time, until thick and glossy. Fold a large spoonful of egg whites into the cooled sauce to loosen the mixture then gently fold in the remaining egg whites.

5 Spoon the mixture into the prepared soufflé dish and bake in a preheated oven, 200°C (400°F), Gas Mark 6, for 25–30 minutes until the soufflé is well risen, the top is browned and there is a slight wobble to the centre.

6 Meanwhile, make the crème anglaise by combining the egg yolks, caster sugar and cornflour, as in Step 2. Bring the milk just to the boil in a small saucepan, then gradually add to the egg yolk mixture. Return the milk mixture to the pan and cook over a medium heat, stirring continuously until thickened and smooth and the custard coats the back of the spoon. Stir in the cream and vanilla essence and set aside.

7 Quickly snip the string off the soufflé collar and gently peel away the paper. Dust the top of the soufflé with sifted drinking chocolate powder and icing sugar and serve immediately, with the warm custard sauce.

classic grand marnier soufflé

butter, for greasing
100 g (3¹/₂ oz) caster sugar, plus
   1 tablespoon for lining the dish
3 egg yolks
40 g (1¹/₂ oz) plain flour
250 ml (8 fl oz) milk
4 tablespoons Grand Marnier
grated rind of 2 oranges
5 egg whites
sifted icing sugar, for dusting

Serves 4
Preparation time: 30 minutes
Cooking time: 22–25 minutes

1 Lightly butter a medium tall 15 cm (6 in) diameter x 9 cm (3³/₄ in) deep soufflé dish, then line the dish with 1 tablespoon caster sugar (see page 8). Attach a soufflé collar that stands 7.5 cm (3 in) higher than the top of the dish (see page 8).

2 Whisk half the remaining caster sugar and the egg yolks in a bowl until thick, pale and mousse-like. Sift the flour over the surface, then gently fold it in.

3 Bring the milk just to the boil in a saucepan, then gradually whisk it into the egg yolk mixture. Return the milk mixture to the pan and cook over a medium heat, stirring continuously until thickened and smooth. Remove from the heat and stir in the Grand Marnier and orange rind. Cover and leave to cool.

4 Whisk the egg whites into stiff, moist-looking peaks. Gradually whisk in the remaining caster sugar, a teaspoon at a time, until thick and glossy. Fold a large spoonful of egg whites into the cooled sauce to loosen the mixture then gently fold in the remaining egg whites.

5 Spoon the mixture into the prepared soufflé dish and bake in a preheated oven, 220°C (425°F), Gas Mark 7, for 17–20 minutes until the soufflé is well risen, the top is browned and there is a slight wobble to the centre. Quickly snip the string off the soufflé collar and gently peel away the paper. Dust the top of the soufflé with sifted icing sugar and serve immediately.

creamy lemon soufflés

butter, for greasing
125 g (4 oz) caster sugar, plus
    4 teaspoons for lining the dishes
3 egg yolks
40 g (1 1/2 oz) plain flour
175 ml (6 fl oz) milk
3 tablespoons double cream
grated rind of 2 lemons
freshly squeezed juice of 1 lemon,
    strained
5 egg whites
sifted icing sugar, for dusting

Serves 4
Preparation time: 30 minutes
Cooking time: 15–17 minutes

Made with storecupboard ingredients, these soufflés are ideal for when you want to transform an everyday meal into something extra special.

1 Lightly butter 4 small 10 cm (4 in) diameter x 6 cm (2 1/2 in) deep soufflé dishes, then line each dish with 1 teaspoon caster sugar (see page 8). Stand the dishes on a baking sheet.

2 Whisk half the remaining caster sugar and the egg yolks in a bowl until thick, pale and mousse-like. Sift the flour over the surface, then gently fold it in.

3 Bring the milk and cream just to the boil in a saucepan, then gradually whisk into the egg yolk mixture. Return the milk mixture to the pan and cook over a medium heat, stirring continuously until thickened and smooth. Beat in the lemon rind and juice, then remove from the heat, cover and leave to cool.

4 Whisk the egg whites into stiff, moist-looking peaks. Gradually whisk in the remaining caster sugar, a teaspoon at a time, until thick and glossy. Fold a large spoonful of egg whites into the cooled sauce to loosen the mixture then gently fold in the remaining egg whites.

5 Spoon the mixture into the prepared soufflé dishes and bake in a preheated oven, 220°C (425°F), Gas Mark 7, for 10–12 minutes until the soufflés are well risen, their tops are browned and there is a slight wobble to the centres. Dust the tops of the soufflés with sifted icing sugar and serve immediately.

warm banana soufflés with choc'n'nut sauce

butter, for greasing
75 g (3 oz) caster sugar, plus
    4 teaspoons for lining the dishes
3 egg yolks
40 g (1 1/2 oz) plain flour
250 ml (8 fl oz) milk
2 small bananas, about 200 g (7 oz)
    in total, weighed with skins on
1 tablespoon lemon juice
1 teaspoon vanilla essence
5 egg whites
sifted icing sugar, for dusting

Hazelnut and chocolate sauce
4 tablespoons chocolate and hazelnut
    spread
4 tablespoons double cream
4 tablespoons milk

Serves 4
Preparation time: 30 minutes
Cooking time: 15–17 minutes

Transform a couple of soft, ripe bananas from the fruit bowl with a few eggs and drizzle with a quick sauce made by heating chocolate and hazelnut spread with cream for a delicious pudding.

1 Lightly butter 4 small 10 cm (4 in) diameter x 6 cm (2 1/2 in) deep soufflé dishes, then line each dish with 1 teaspoon caster sugar (see page 8). Stand the dishes on a baking sheet.

2 Whisk half the remaining caster sugar and the egg yolks in a bowl until thick, pale and mousse-like. Sift the flour over the surface, then gently fold it in.

3 Bring the milk just to the boil in a saucepan, then gradually whisk it into the egg yolk mixture. Return the milk mixture to the pan and cook over a medium heat, stirring continuously until thickened and smooth. Remove from the heat, cover and leave to cool.

4 Mash the bananas with the lemon juice, then stir into the cooled sauce with the vanilla essence. Whisk the egg whites into stiff, moist-looking peaks. Gradually whisk in the remaining caster sugar, a teaspoon at a time, until thick and glossy. Fold a large spoonful of egg whites into the cooled sauce to loosen the mixture then gently fold in the remaining egg whites.

5 Spoon the mixture into the prepared soufflé dishes and bake in a preheated oven, 220°C (425°F), Gas Mark 7, for 10–12 minutes until the soufflés are well risen, their tops are browned and there is a slight wobble to the centres.

6 Meanwhile, gently heat all the sauce ingredients together in a small saucepan, stirring until smooth, then pour into a serving jug. Dust the tops of the soufflés with sifted icing sugar and serve immediately, with the warmed sauce poured into the centre of each one.

papaya, kiwi, fig and lime soufflé

Sweet perfumed papaya, colourful green wedges of kiwifruit and fresh figs are bathed in a frothy hot lime and coconut soufflé. The mixture could be cooked in a medium tall 15 cm (6 in) diameter x 9 cm (3 3/4 in) deep soufflé dish with the fruits served as a side dish, if preferred.

1 Lightly butter a 1.5 litre (3 pint), 4 cm (1 1/2 in) deep ovenproof dish, then line the dish with 1 tablespoon caster sugar (see page 8). Arrange the fruits at angles in the base of the dish.

2 Whisk half the remaining caster sugar and the egg yolks in a bowl until thick, pale and mousse-like. Sift the flour over the surface, then gently fold it in.

3 Bring the milk just to the boil in a saucepan, then gradually whisk it into the egg yolk mixture. Return the milk mixture to the pan and cook over a medium heat, stirring continuously until thickened and smooth. Stir in the lime rind and juice, cover and leave to cool.

4 Whisk the egg whites into stiff, moist-looking peaks. Gradually whisk in the remaining caster sugar, a teaspoon at a time, until thick and glossy. Fold a large spoonful of egg whites into the cooled sauce to loosen the mixture then gently fold in the remaining egg whites.

5 Spoon the mixture into the fruit-filled dish, sprinkle with desiccated coconut and bake in a preheated oven, 200°C (400°F), Gas Mark 6, for 12–15 minutes until the soufflé is well risen, the top is browned and there is a slight wobble to the centre. Dust the top of the soufflé with sifted icing sugar and serve immediately.

butter, for greasing
125 g (4 oz) caster sugar, plus
   1 tablespoon for lining the dish
1 ripe papaya, halved, seeds removed,
   peeled and sliced
2 kiwifruit, peeled and cut into wedges
2 fresh figs, quartered and peeled
3 egg yolks
40 g (1 1/2 oz) plain flour
250 ml (8 fl oz) milk
grated rind and juice of 2 limes
5 egg whites
2 tablespoons desiccated coconut
sifted icing sugar, for dusting

Serves 4
Preparation time: 30 minutes
Cooking time: 15–17 minutes

berry soufflés with red berry coulis

butter, for greasing
125 g (4 oz) caster sugar, plus
    4 teaspoons for lining the dishes
3 egg yolks
40 g (1½ oz) plain flour
250 ml (8 fl oz) milk
grated rind of ½ lemon
5 egg whites
150 g (5 oz) mixed red berry fruits,
    defrosted if frozen, plus extra
    to serve
sifted icing sugar, for dusting

Coulis
300 g (10 oz) raspberries, defrosted
    if frozen
2 tablespoons caster sugar

Serves 4
Preparation time: 30 minutes
Cooking time: 15–17 minutes

Dotted with whole berry fruits, this delicate, airy soufflé is served with a speedy puréed fruit sauce lightly sweetened to taste.

1 Lightly butter 4 small 10 cm (4 in) diameter x 6 cm (2½ in) deep glass dishes, then line each dish with 1 teaspoon caster sugar (see page 8). Stand the dishes on a baking sheet.

2 Whisk half the remaining caster sugar and the egg yolks in a bowl until thick, pale and mousse-like. Sift the flour over the surface, then gently fold it in.

3 Bring the milk just to the boil in a saucepan, then gradually whisk it into the egg yolk mixture. Return the milk mixture to the pan and cook over a medium heat, stirring continuously until thickened and smooth. Stir in the lemon rind, cover and leave to cool.

4 Whisk the egg whites into stiff, moist-looking peaks. Gradually whisk in the remaining caster sugar, a teaspoon at a time, until thick and glossy. Fold a large spoonful of egg whites into the cooled sauce to loosen the mixture then gently fold in the remaining egg whites, followed by the mixed berries.

5 Spoon the mixture into the prepared glass dishes and bake in a preheated oven, 220°C (425°F), Gas Mark 7, for 10–12 minutes until the soufflés are well risen, their tops are browned and there is a slight wobble to the centres. Meanwhile, make the coulis by puréeing the raspberries in a liquidizer or food processor, press through a sieve into a bowl then stir in the caster sugar.

6 Dust the tops of the soufflés with sifted icing sugar and serve immediately, with the raspberry coulis and extra mixed berries.

hazelnut soufflés

butter, for greasing
2 tablespoons ground almonds
50 g (2 oz) caster sugar
50 g (2 oz) light muscovado sugar
3 egg yolks
40 g (1 1/2 oz) plain flour
250 ml (8 fl oz) milk
50 g (2 oz) hazelnuts, plus extra
   roughly chopped, to decorate
5 egg whites
sifted icing sugar, for dusting

Serves 4
Preparation time: 30 minutes
Cooking time: 15–17 minutes

Hazelnuts are much less frequently used than other nuts, yet they have a stronger, more mellow taste, especially when toasted first. These soufflés are delicious served with crème anglaise or chocolate sauce (see page 34 or 32).

1 Lightly butter 4 small 10 cm (4 in) diameter x 6 cm (2 1/2 in) deep soufflé dishes, then line each dish with 1/2 tablespoon ground almonds (see page 8). Stand the dishes on a baking sheet.

2 Mix the sugars together, then whisk half in a bowl with the egg yolks until thick, pale and mousse-like. Sift the flour over the surface, then gently fold it in.

3 Bring the milk just to the boil in a saucepan, then gradually whisk it into the egg yolk mixture. Return the milk mixture to the pan and cook over a medium heat, stirring continuously until thickened and smooth.

4 Place the whole hazelnuts on a piece of foil and toast under the grill until lightly browned. Finely chop, then stir into the sauce. Cover and leave to cool.

5 Whisk the egg whites into stiff, moist-looking peaks. Gradually whisk in the remaining sugar, a teaspoon at a time, until thick and glossy. Fold a large spoonful of egg whites into the cooled sauce to loosen the mixture then gently fold in the remaining egg whites.

6 Spoon the mixture into the prepared soufflé dishes, sprinkle with the roughly chopped hazelnuts and bake in a preheated oven, 220°C (425°F), Gas Mark 7, for 10–12 minutes until the soufflés are well risen, their tops are browned and there is a slight wobble to the centres. Dust the top of the soufflés liberally with sifted icing sugar and serve immediately.

apple soufflé with cinnamon cream

This light, delicate, fruit-flavoured soufflé is made with sharp cooking apples and complemented by a smooth, creamy sauce that can be stirred together in a matter of seconds.

1   Lightly butter a medium tall 15 cm (6 in) diameter x 9 cm (3³/4 in) deep soufflé dish, then line the dish with the ground almonds (see page 8). Attach a soufflé collar that stands 7.5 cm (3 in) higher than the top of the dish (see page 8).

2   Place the apple slices in a small saucepan with the water. Cover and cook gently for 5 minutes or until pulpy.

3   Mix the sugars together, then whisk half in a bowl with the egg yolks until thick, pale and mousse-like. Sift the flour over the surface, then gently fold it in.

4   Bring the milk just to the boil in a saucepan, then gradually whisk it into the egg yolk mixture. Return the milk mixture to the pan and cook over a medium heat, stirring continuously until thickened and smooth. Stir in the cooked apple and the ground cinnamon, cover and leave to cool.

5   Whisk the egg whites into stiff, moist-looking peaks. Gradually whisk in the remaining sugar, a teaspoon at a time, until thick and glossy. Fold a large spoonful of egg whites into the cooled sauce to loosen the mixture then gently fold in the remaining egg whites.

6   Spoon the mixture into the prepared soufflé dish and bake in a preheated oven, 220°C (425°F), Gas Mark 7, for about 20 minutes until the soufflé is well risen, the top is browned and there is a slight wobble to the centre. Meanwhile, stir the sauce ingredients together and gently warm, if liked.

7   When cooked, dust the top of the soufflé with sifted icing sugar, snip the string off the soufflé collar and gently peel away the paper. Spoon the soufflé into dishes and serve immediately with the cream sauce drizzled over.

butter, for greasing
1 tablespoon ground almonds
1 cooking apple, about 275 g (9 oz),
   quartered, cored, peeled and
   thinly sliced
1 tablespoon water
50 g (2 oz) caster sugar
50 g (2 oz) light muscovado sugar
3 egg yolks
40 g (1¹/2 oz) plain flour
250 ml (8 fl oz) milk
1/8 teaspoon ground cinnamon
5 egg whites
sifted icing sugar, for dusting

Cinnamon cream sauce
250 ml (8 fl oz) double cream
2 teaspoons light muscovado sugar
2 large pinches of ground cinnamon

Serves 4
Preparation time: 30 minutes
Cooking time: 30 minutes

cranberry and orange soufflés

butter, for greasing
100 g (3½ oz) caster sugar, plus
    4 teaspoons for lining the dishes
75 g (3 oz) dried cranberries
grated rind of 2 oranges
3 tablespoons freshly squeezed
    orange juice
3 egg yolks
40 g (1½ oz) plain flour
250 ml (8 fl oz) milk
5 egg whites
sifted icing sugar, for dusting
orange rind curls, to decorate (see
    page 57)

Serves 4
Preparation time: 30 minutes, plus
    standing
Cooking time: 15–17 minutes

Serve these soufflés with cream or crème fraîche flavoured with a little Cointreau, if liked. Use 125 g (4 oz) fresh cranberries instead of the dried fruit, if preferred – cook them with the orange rind, juice and 2 tablespoons water until the berries have softened. Leave to cool, then fold into the cooled sauce at Step 5, as below.

1 Lightly butter 4 small 10 cm (4 in) diameter x 6 cm (2½ in) deep soufflé dishes, then line each dish with 1 teaspoon caster sugar (see page 8). Stand the dishes on a baking sheet.

2 Warm the dried cranberries, orange rind and juice together in a small saucepan. Remove from the heat and leave the cranberries to plump up for about 30 minutes.

3 Whisk half the remaining caster sugar and the egg yolks in a bowl until thick, pale and mousse-like. Sift the flour over the surface, then gently fold it in.

4 Bring the milk just to the boil in a saucepan, then gradually whisk it into the egg yolk mixture. Return the milk mixture to the pan and cook over a medium heat, stirring continuously until thickened and smooth. Cover and leave to cool.

5 Whisk the egg whites into stiff, moist-looking peaks. Gradually whisk in the remaining caster sugar, a teaspoon at a time, until thick and glossy. Fold a large spoonful of egg whites into the cooled sauce to loosen the mixture then mix in the soaked cranberries. Gently fold in the remaining egg whites.

6 Spoon the mixture into the prepared soufflé dishes and bake in a preheated oven, 220°C (425°F), Gas Mark 7, for 10–12 minutes until the soufflés are well risen, their tops are browned and there is a slight wobble to the centres. Dust the tops of the soufflés with icing sugar and decorate with orange rind curls. Serve immediately.

twice-baked cappuccino soufflés

butter, for greasing
3 egg yolks
75 g (3 oz) golden caster sugar
40 g (1 1/2 oz) plain flour
250 ml (8 fl oz) milk
2 teaspoons instant coffee granules
   or powder
2 egg whites

To finish
250 ml (8 fl oz) double cream
3 tablespoons golden caster sugar
1 teaspoon instant coffee granules or
   powder
2 tablespoons brandy or whisky
   (optional)
75 g (3 oz) dark chocolate, broken into
   pieces
sifted drinking chocolate powder,
   for dusting

Serves 6
Preparation time: 30 minutes
Cooking time: 20 minutes, plus cooling
Reheating time: 12–15 minutes

Reminiscent of a light coffee custard, these double-baked soufflés are first baked in ramekins, then turned out, drizzled with cream and reheated before being served with a creamy coffee sauce and dusted with drinking chocolate powder for an authentic cappuccino finish.

1 Lightly butter 6 individual 7.5 cm (3 in) diameter x 4 cm (1 1/2 in) deep soufflé dishes, then stand them on a rack in a roasting tin.

2 Whisk the egg yolks and caster sugar in a bowl until thick, pale and mousse-like. Sift the flour over the surface, then gently fold it in.

3 Bring the milk just to the boil in a saucepan, then gradually whisk it into the egg yolk mixture. Return the milk mixture to the pan and cook over a medium heat, stirring continuously until thickened and smooth. Stir in the instant coffee until dissolved. Cover and leave to cool for 15 minutes.

4 Whisk the egg whites into stiff, moist-looking peaks. Fold a large spoonful into the cooled sauce to loosen the mixture then fold in the remaining egg whites.

5 Spoon the mixture into the prepared soufflé dishes and pour hot water into the roasting tin to come halfway up the sides of the dishes. Bake, uncovered, in a preheated oven, 180°C (350°F), Gas Mark 4, for 15 minutes until the soufflés are well risen and spongy to the touch. Lift the dishes out of the tin and allow to cool slightly. Then run a knife around the edges and unmould the soufflés, with the tops uppermost, into a buttered shallow ovenproof dish, leaving a little room between them.

6 When ready to reheat, drizzle 1 tablespoon cream over each soufflé and sprinkle each one with 1/2 teaspoon of the sugar. Bake, uncovered, in a preheated oven, 180°C (350°F), Gas Mark 4, for 12–15 minutes until hot and slightly puffed up.

7 Meanwhile, warm the remaining cream and the remaining sugar in a small saucepan until the sugar has dissolved. Stir in the coffee and brandy or whisky, if using. Melt the chocolate in a bowl over hot water, then spoon into a paper piping bag and snip off the tip. Pipe squiggly lines around the edges of 6 serving plates.

8 Drizzle the coffee sauce inside the chocolate line on each plate. Add the reheated soufflés, quickly dust with drinking chocolate and serve immediately.

individual lemon and vodka soufflés

4 tablespoons cold water

4 teaspoons powdered gelatine

4 eggs, separated

175 g (6 oz) caster sugar

finely grated rind of 2½ lemons

150 ml (¼ pint) strained freshly
   squeezed lemon juice

4 tablespoons vodka

250 ml (8 fl oz) double cream

To decorate

125 ml (4 fl oz) double cream, whipped

lemon rind curls (see page 57)

roughly chopped pistachio nuts

Serves 6

Preparation time: 30 minutes, plus
   chilling

Cooking time: 13–14 minutes

1 Attach soufflé collars to 6 individual 7.5 cm (3 in) diameter x 4 cm (1½ in) deep soufflé dishes so that the paper stands 4 cm (1½ in) higher than the top of each dish (see page 8). Stand the dishes on a tray.

2 Put the water in a small heatproof bowl or mug and sprinkle over the gelatine, making sure that the water absorbs all the powder. Set aside for 5 minutes, then stand the bowl in a small saucepan half-filled with boiling water and simmer for 3–4 minutes, stirring occasionally, until the gelatine dissolves to a clear liquid.

3 Put the egg yolks, sugar and lemon rind in a large heatproof bowl then stand the bowl over a saucepan of simmering water so that the base of the bowl is not touching the water. Whisk using a hand-held electric whisk for about 10 minutes until the eggs are very thick and pale, and the whisk leaves a trail when lifted above the mixture.

4 Gradually whisk in the strained lemon juice and continue whisking until thick once more. Remove the bowl from the heat and continue whisking until cool.

5 Gradually fold in the dissolved gelatine, adding it in a thin, steady stream, then fold in the vodka.

6 Softly whip the cream (no need to wash the whisk in between), then fold into the soufflé mixture. Chill if the mixture is very soft.

7 Wash the whisk and dry it well then use it to whisk the egg whites into stiff, moist-looking peaks. Fold a large spoonful into the soufflé mixture to loosen it then gently fold in the remaining egg whites. Pour the mixture into the prepared soufflé dishes so that it stands above the rim of the dishes. Chill for 4 hours or until set.

8 To serve, snip the string off the soufflé collars and gently peel away the paper. Add a spoonful of whipped cream to the centre of each soufflé and top with lemon rind curls and a few chopped pistachio nuts. Return to the refrigerator and serve within 30 minutes.

marbled blueberry and white chocolate souffl

4 tablespoons water
4 teaspoons powdered gelatine
4 eggs, separated
150 g (5 oz) caster sugar
250 ml (8 fl oz) double cream
300 g (10 oz) blueberries, defrosted
   if frozen, puréed and pressed
   through a sieve
125 g (4 oz) white chocolate, melted

Serves 6
Preparation time: 40 minutes, plus
   chilling
Cooking time: 13–14 minutes

1 Attach soufflé collars to 6 individual 7.5 cm (3 in) diameter x 4 cm (1 1/2 in) deep glass dishes so that the paper stands 4 cm (1 1/2 in) higher than the top of each dish (see page 8). Stand the dishes on a tray.

2 Put the water in a small heatproof bowl or mug and sprinkle over the gelatine, making sure that the water absorbs all the powder. Set aside for 5 minutes, then stand the bowl in a small saucepan half-filled with boiling water and simmer for 3–4 minutes, stirring occasionally, until the gelatine dissolves to a clear liquid.

3 Put the egg yolks and sugar in a large heatproof bowl, then stand the bowl over a saucepan of simmering water so that the base of the bowl is not touching the water. Whisk using a hand-held electric whisk for about 10 minutes until the eggs are very thick and pale and the whisk leaves a trail when lifted above the mixture. Remove the bowl from the heat and continue whisking until cool.

4 Gradually fold in the dissolved gelatine, adding it in a thin, steady stream. Softly whip the cream (no need to wash the whisk in between), then fold into the soufflé mixture.

5 Spoon one-third of the mixture into a separate bowl and fold in the sieved blueberry purée. Fold the melted chocolate into the remaining mixture in the original bowl.

6 Wash the whisk and dry it well, then use it to whisk the egg whites into stiff, moist-looking peaks. Fold a spoonful into each bowl of chocolate and blueberry soufflé mixture to loosen then gently fold in the remaining egg whites, adding one-third to the blueberry mixture and the rest to the chocolate mixture.

7 Add alternate spoonfuls of each soufflé mixture to the prepared glass dishes so that they stand above the rim of the dishes. Run a knife through the mixtures to create a marbled effect, then chill for 4 hours or overnight until set. To serve, snip the string off the soufflé collars and gently peel away the paper.

chilled blackcurrant and mint soufflé

250 g (8 oz) blackcurrants, defrosted
   if frozen
6 tablespoons water
4 teaspoons powdered gelatine
4 eggs, separated
200 g (7 oz) caster sugar
250 ml (8 fl oz) double cream
5 tablespoons finely chopped mint
4 teaspoons sifted icing sugar, for
   dusting

Serves 6
Preparation time: 40 minutes, plus
   chilling
Cooking time: 18–19 minutes

1 Attach a soufflé collar to a small 13 cm (5^1/$_2$ in) diameter x 6 cm (2^1/$_2$ in) deep soufflé dish so that the paper stands 6 cm (2^1/$_2$ in) higher than the top of the dish (see page 8).

2 Put the blackcurrants in a small saucepan with 2 tablespoons of the water, cover and cook gently for 5 minutes until softened. Blend in a liquidizer or food processor until smooth then press through a sieve.

3 Meanwhile, put the remaining water in a small heatproof bowl or mug and sprinkle over the gelatine, making sure that the water absorbs all the powder. Set aside for 5 minutes, then stand the bowl in a small saucepan half-filled with boiling water and simmer for 3–4 minutes, stirring occasionally, until the gelatine dissolves to a clear liquid.

4 Put the egg yolks and caster sugar in a large heatproof bowl, then stand the bowl over a saucepan of simmering water so that the base of the bowl is not touching the water. Whisk using a hand-held electric whisk for about 10 minutes until the eggs are very thick and pale, and the whisk leaves a trail when lifted above the mixture. Remove the bowl from the heat and continue whisking until cool.

5 Gradually fold in the dissolved gelatine, adding it in a thin, steady stream, then fold in the blackcurrant purée.

6 Softly whip the cream (no need to wash the whisk in between), then fold into the soufflé mixture with the chopped mint.

7 Wash the whisk and dry it well then use it to whisk the egg whites into stiff, moist-looking peaks. Fold a large spoonful into the soufflé mixture to loosen it, then gently fold in the remaining egg whites. Pour the mixture into the prepared soufflé dish so that it stands above the rim of the dish. Chill for 4 hours or until set.

8 To serve, snip the string off the soufflé collar and gently peel away the paper. Arrange 4 or 5 curved strips of nonstick baking paper about 1 inch (2.5 cm) wide over the soufflé top so that some overlap, then dust with sifted icing sugar. Carefully lift off the paper strips and serve immediately or the sugar will dissolve and disappear.

cherry and amaretto soufflé

Speckled with crushed almond-flavoured Italian amaretti biscuits, this soufflé is set around a jam jar, which is later removed to leave a cavity ready to be filled with canned cherries.

4 tablespoons water

4 teaspoons powdered gelatine

4 eggs, separated

125 g (4 oz) caster sugar

125 g (4 oz) amaretti biscuits, finely crushed

250 ml (8 fl oz) double cream, softly whipped

3 tablespoons Amaretto liqueur

425 g (14 oz) canned pitted black cherries, drained

Serves 6

Preparation time: 40 minutes, plus chilling

Cooking time: 13–14 minutes

1 Attach a soufflé collar to a medium 16.5 cm (6³/4 in) diameter x 7.5 cm (3 in) deep soufflé dish so that the paper stands 7.5 cm (3 in) higher than the top of the dish (see page 8). Stand a tall 6 cm (2¹/2 in) diameter jam jar in the centre of the dish to create a ring mould shape.

2 Put the water in a small heatproof bowl or mug and sprinkle over the gelatine, making sure that the water absorbs all the powder. Set aside for 5 minutes, then stand the bowl in a small saucepan half-filled with boiling water and simmer for 3–4 minutes, stirring occasionally, until the gelatine dissolves to a clear liquid.

3 Put the egg yolks and sugar in a large heatproof bowl, then stand the bowl over a saucepan of simmering water so that the base of the bowl is not touching the water. Whisk using a hand-held electric whisk for about 10 minutes until the eggs are very thick and pale, and the whisk leaves a trail when lifted above the mixture. Remove the bowl from the heat and continue whisking until cool.

4 Gradually fold in the dissolved gelatine, adding it in a thin, steady stream. Reserve one-quarter of the crushed biscuits for decoration and fold the rest into the egg yolk mixture with the whipped cream and Amaretto.

5 Wash the whisk and dry it well then use it to whisk the egg whites into stiff, moist-looking peaks. Fold a large spoonful into the soufflé mixture to loosen it then gently fold in the remaining egg whites. Pour the mixture into the prepared soufflé dish so that it stands above the rim of the dish, but avoids the top of the jar. Chill for 4 hours or until set.

6 To serve, pour a little hot water into the jam jar, leave for a few seconds, then gently twist the jar and remove. Snip the string off the soufflé collar and gently peel away the paper. Fill the central cavity with the drained cherries and press the remaining biscuit crumbs around the outside of the soufflé before serving.

gingered apple soufflés

500 g (1 lb) cooking apples, peeled, cored and sliced
8 tablespoons water
4 teaspoons powdered gelatine
4 eggs, separated
150 g (5 oz) caster sugar
250 ml (8 fl oz) double cream
3 teaspoons chopped glacé, crystallized or drained stem ginger

To decorate
125 ml (4 fl oz) double cream, whipped
1/2 red dessert apple, cored, thinly sliced and dipped in lemon juice

Serves 6
Preparation time: 40 minutes, plus chilling
Cooking time: 23–24 minutes

These light and creamy, smooth chilled soufflés are a mix of comforting, traditionally partnered flavours.

1 Attach soufflé collars to 6 individual 7.5 cm (3 in) diameter x 4 cm (1 1/2 in) deep soufflé dishes so that the paper stands 4 cm (1 1/2 in) higher than the top of each dish (see page 8). Stand the dishes on a tray.

2 Put the apples and half the water in a saucepan, cover and simmer for 10 minutes until soft. Mash with a fork if necessary. Leave to cool.

3 Put the remaining water in a small heatproof bowl or mug and sprinkle over the gelatine, making sure that the water absorbs all the powder. Set aside for 5 minutes, then stand the bowl in a small saucepan half-filled with boiling water and simmer for 3–4 minutes, stirring occasionally, until the gelatine dissolves to a clear liquid.

4 Put the egg yolks and caster sugar in a large heatproof bowl, then stand the bowl over a saucepan of simmering water so that the base of the bowl is not touching the water. Whisk using a hand-held electric whisk for about 10 minutes until the eggs are very thick and pale, and the whisk leaves a trail when lifted above the mixture. Remove the bowl from the heat and continue whisking until cool.

5 Gradually fold in the dissolved gelatine, adding it in a thin, steady stream, then fold in the apples.

6 Softly whip the cream (no need to wash the whisk in between), then fold into the soufflé mixture with the ginger.

7 Wash the whisk and dry it well then use it to whisk the egg whites into stiff, moist-looking peaks. Fold a large spoonful into the soufflé mixture to loosen it then gently fold in the remaining egg whites. Pour the mixture into the prepared soufflé dishes so that it stands above the rim of the dishes. Chill for 4 hours or until set.

8 To serve, snip the string off the soufflé collars and gently peel away the paper. Spoon or pipe whipped cream into the centre of each soufflé and top with thin slices of apple.

strawberry and lavender soufflés

500 g (1 lb) fresh strawberries, hulled

4 tablespoons water

4 teaspoons powdered gelatine

4 eggs, separated

150 g (5 oz) caster sugar

4–5 lavender sprigs, petals crumbled,
stems discarded

250 ml (8 fl oz) double cream

a few drops of pink or red food
colouring (optional)

small bunch of lavender, to decorate

Serves 6

Preparation time: 40 minutes, plus
chilling

Cooking time: 13–14 minutes

Subtly flavoured with just a hint of fresh lavender, these delicate strawberry soufflés seem to encapsulate the very essence of summer.

1 Attach soufflé collars to 6 individual 7.5 cm (3 in) diameter x 4 cm (1¹/₂ in) deep soufflé dishes so that the paper stands 4 cm (1¹/₂ in) higher than the top of each dish (see page 8). Stand the dishes on a tray.

2 Slice 6 strawberries and divide them between the bases of the soufflé dishes. Blend the remaining strawberries to a coarse purée in a liquidizer or food processor, or using a potato masher.

3 Put the water in a small heatproof bowl or mug and sprinkle over the gelatine, making sure that the water absorbs all the powder. Set aside for 5 minutes, then stand the bowl in a small saucepan half-filled with boiling water and simmer for 3–4 minutes, stirring occasionally, until the gelatine dissolves to a clear liquid.

4 Put the egg yolks, sugar and lavender petals in a large heatproof bowl, then stand the bowl over a saucepan of simmering water so that the base of the bowl is not touching the water. Whisk using a hand-held electric whisk for about 10 minutes until the eggs are very thick and pale, and the whisk leaves a trail when lifted above the mixture. Remove the bowl from the heat and continue whisking until cool.

5 Gradually fold in the dissolved gelatine, adding it in a thin, steady stream, then fold in the strawberry purée.

6 Softly whip the cream (no need to wash the whisk in between), then fold into the soufflé mixture with the food colouring, if using. Chill if the mixture is very soft.

7 Wash the whisk and dry it well then use it to whisk the egg whites into stiff, moist-looking peaks. Fold a large spoonful into the soufflé mixture to loosen it then gently fold in the remaining egg whites. Pour the mixture into the prepared soufflé dishes so that it stands above the rim of the dishes. Chill for 4 hours or until set.

8 To serve, peel back the paper collars and tuck a few trimmed lavender stems under the string.

rhubarb and clotted cream soufflés

750 g (1 1/2 lb) trimmed rhubarb, sliced
8 tablespoons water
200 g (7 oz) caster sugar
4 teaspoons powdered gelatine
4 eggs, separated
200 g (7 oz) clotted cream
a few drops of pink food colouring
    (optional)

To decorate
100 g (3 1/2 oz) clotted cream
mint leaves

Serves 6
Preparation time: 40 minutes, plus
    chilling
Cooking time: 18–19 minutes

Spoon down through the rich, creamy smoothness of these pretty pink soufflés to find a surprise fruity layer beneath. If you are using rhubarb later in the season when its colour is not so good, add a few drops of pink food colouring to the soufflé mixture when adding the egg whites.

1 Attach soufflé collars to 6 individual 7.5 cm (3 in) diameter x 4 cm (1 1/2 in) deep soufflé dishes so that the paper stands 4 cm (1 1/2 in) higher than the top of each dish (see page 8). Stand the dishes on a tray.

2 Put the rhubarb in a saucepan with half the water, cover and simmer for 5 minutes until softened but still bright pink. Break up any large pieces with a fork, then spoon one-third of the rhubarb into a bowl and sweeten with 25 g (1 oz) of the sugar. Divide between the bases of the prepared soufflé dishes.

3 Put the remaining water in a small heatproof bowl or mug and sprinkle over the gelatine, making sure that the water absorbs all the powder. Set aside for 5 minutes, then stand the bowl in a small saucepan half-filled with boiling water and simmer for 3–4 minutes, stirring occasionally, until the gelatine dissolves to a clear liquid.

4 Put the egg yolks and remaining sugar in a large bowl then stand the bowl over a saucepan of simmering water so that the base of the bowl is not touching the water. Whisk using a hand-held electric whisk for about 10 minutes until the eggs are very thick and pale, and the whisk leaves a trail when lifted above the mixture. Remove the bowl from the heat and continue whisking until cool.

5 Gradually fold in the dissolved gelatine, adding it in a thin, steady stream, then fold in the remaining cooked rhubarb and the clotted cream. Chill for 30 minutes if the mixture is very soft.

6 Wash the whisk and dry it well then use it to whisk the egg whites into stiff, moist-looking peaks. Fold a large spoonful into the soufflé mixture to loosen it then gently fold in the remaining egg whites and the colouring, if using. Pour the mixture into the prepared soufflé dishes so that it stands above the rim of the dishes. Chill for 4 hours or until set.

7 To serve, snip the string off the soufflé collars and gently peel away the paper. Top each soufflé with a spoonful of clotted cream and a mint leaf.

honeyed crème fraîche and orange soufflé

4 tablespoons water

4 teaspoons powdered gelatine

4 eggs, separated

125 g (4 oz) thick-set flower or lavender
   honey

grated rind of 1 orange

5 tablespoons freshly squeezed orange
   juice

300 ml (1/2 pint) half-fat crème fraîche

orange rind curls (see method),
   to decorate

Serves 6

Preparation time: 40 minutes, plus
   chilling

Cooking time: 13–14 minutes

*This very delicately flavoured soufflé is only as good as the honey that you use,
so choose a thick-set mixed flower or lavender honey, if possible. Serve the
soufflé on its own or with pears simmered in cider.*

1 Attach a soufflé collar to a small 13 cm (5$^{1}/_{2}$ in) diameter x 6 cm (2$^{1}/_{2}$ in) deep
   soufflé dish so that the paper stands 6 cm (2$^{1}/_{2}$ in) higher than the top of the
   dish (see page 8).

2 Put the water in a small heatproof bowl or mug and sprinkle over the gelatine,
   making sure that the water absorbs all the powder. Set aside for 5 minutes,
   then stand the bowl in a small saucepan half-filled with boiling water and
   simmer for 3–4 minutes, stirring occasionally, until the gelatine dissolves to
   a clear liquid.

3 Put the egg yolks, honey and orange rind in a large heatproof bowl, then stand
   the bowl over a saucepan of simmering water so that the base of the bowl is not
   touching the water. Whisk using a hand-held electric whisk for about 10 minutes
   until the eggs are very thick and pale, and the whisk leaves a trail when lifted
   above the mixture.

4 Gradually whisk in the orange juice and whisk until thick once more. Remove
   the bowl from the heat and continue whisking until cool.

5 Gradually fold in the dissolved gelatine, adding it in a thin, steady stream, then
   fold in the crème fraîche. Chill for 20–30 minutes if the mixture is very soft.

6 Wash the whisk and dry it well then use it to whisk the egg whites into stiff,
   moist-looking peaks. Fold a large spoonful into the soufflé mixture to loosen it
   then gently fold in the remaining egg whites. Pour the mixture into the prepared
   soufflé dish so that it stands above the rim of the dish. Chill for 4 hours or
   until set.

7 To serve, snip the string off the soufflé collar and gently peel away the paper.
   Top with orange rind curls, made by paring the rind from an orange, then
   winding the long strips around a skewer and holding in place for a minute or so.

passion fruit and lime soufflé

4 tablespoons water

4 teaspoons powdered gelatine

4 eggs, separated

175 g (6 oz) caster sugar

grated rind of 3 limes

5 tablespoons freshly squeezed
lime juice

8 passion fruit, halved

250 ml (8 fl oz) double cream

Serves 6
Preparation time: 40 minutes, plus
chilling
Cooking time: 13–14 minutes

*Passion fruit add the most wonderful exotic perfume and intense flavour to this
light, frothy, lime soufflé. It is not true that the wrinklier they are the better, they
are simply older fruits.*

1 Attach a soufflé collar to a small 13 cm (5$\frac{1}{2}$ in) diameter x 6 cm (2$\frac{1}{2}$ in) deep
soufflé dish so that the paper stands 6 cm (2$\frac{1}{2}$ in) higher than the top of the
dish (see page 8).

2 Put the water in a small heatproof bowl or mug and sprinkle over the gelatine,
making sure that the water absorbs all the powder. Set aside for 5 minutes, then
stand the bowl in a small saucepan half-filled with boiling water and simmer for
3–4 minutes, stirring occasionally, until the gelatine dissolves to a clear liquid.

3 Put the egg yolks, sugar and lime rind in a large heatproof bowl, then stand the
bowl over a saucepan of simmering water so that the base of the bowl is not
touching the water. Whisk using a hand-held electric whisk for about 10 minutes
until the eggs are very thick and pale, and the whisk leaves a trail when lifted
above the mixture.

4 Gradually whisk in the lime juice and whisk until thick once more. Remove the
bowl from the heat and continue whisking until cool.

5 Gradually fold in the dissolved gelatine, adding it in a thin, steady stream.
Scoop the seeds out of 6 of the passion fruit and fold into the soufflé mixture.

6 Softly whip the cream (no need to wash the whisk in between), then fold into
the soufflé mixture and chill for 20–30 minutes until just beginning to set. Lightly
stir the mixture once more to redistribute any passion fruit seeds that may have
sunk to the bottom.

7 Wash the whisk and dry it well then use it to whisk the egg whites into stiff,
moist-looking peaks. Fold a large spoonful into the soufflé mixture to loosen
it then gently fold in the remaining egg whites. Pour the mixture into the
prepared soufflé dish so that it stands above the rim of the dish. Chill for
4 hours or until set.

8 To serve, snip the string off the soufflé collar and gently peel away the paper.
Top the soufflé with seeds scooped from the remaining 2 passion fruit.

coffee and cinnamon latte soufflés

4 tablespoons water

4 teaspoons powdered gelatine

4 eggs, separated

175 g (6 oz) soft light muscovado sugar

1 teaspoon ground cinnamon

175 ml (6 fl oz) strong black coffee,
   cooled

250 ml (8 fl oz) double cream

3 tablespoons whisky or brandy
   (optional)

To decorate
chocolate-covered coffee beans
sifted icing sugar, for dusting

Serves 6
Preparation time: 30 minutes, plus
   chilling
Cooking time: 13–14 minutes

Use either leftover coffee from the cafetière or percolator, or make up some strong instant coffee with the tiniest amount of boiling water and top up with cold. Bring out the flavour with a hint of cinnamon and some moist muscovado sugar.

1 Attach soufflé collars to 6 individual 7.5 cm (3 in) diameter x 4 cm (1½ in) deep soufflé dishes so that the paper stands 4 cm (1½ in) higher than the top of each dish (see page 8). Stand the dishes on a tray.

2 Put the water in a small heatproof bowl or mug and sprinkle over the gelatine, making sure that the water absorbs all the powder. Set aside for 5 minutes, then stand the bowl in a small saucepan half-filled with boiling water and simmer for 3–4 minutes, stirring occasionally, until the gelatine dissolves to a clear liquid.

3 Put the egg yolks, brown sugar and cinnamon in a large heatproof bowl, then stand the bowl over a saucepan of simmering water so that the base of the bowl is not touching the water. Whisk using a hand-held electric whisk for about 10 minutes until the eggs are very thick and pale, and the whisk leaves a trail when lifted above the mixture.

4 Remove the bowl from the heat, gradually whisk in the coffee and continue whisking until the soufflé mixture is cool. Gradually fold in the dissolved gelatine, adding it in a thin, steady stream.

5 Softly whip the cream (no need to wash the whisk in between), then fold into the soufflé mixture with the whisky or brandy, if using. Chill for 30 minutes if the mixture is very soft.

6 Wash the whisk and dry it well then use it to whisk the egg whites into stiff, moist-looking peaks. Fold a large spoonful into the soufflé mixture to loosen it then gently fold in the remaining egg whites. Pour the mixture into the prepared soufflé dishes so that it stands above the rim of the dishes. Chill for 4 hours or until set.

7 To serve, snip the string off the soufflé collars and gently peel away the paper. Top each soufflé with a few coffee beans and a dusting of icing sugar.

brandied chocolate and chestnut soufflé

3 tablespoons water

3 teaspoons powdered gelatine

4 eggs, separated

125 g (4 oz) caster sugar

250 g (8 oz) can sweetened chestnut
    purée

3 tablespoons brandy

125 g (4 oz) plain dark chocolate,
    melted

175 ml (6 fl oz) double cream

dark chocolate curls (see method),
    to decorate

Serves 6

Preparation time: 30 minutes, plus
    chilling

Cooking time: 13–14 minutes

This velvety smooth, rich chocolate soufflé with just a hint of chestnut is the perfect choice for a special Christmas meal.

1 Attach a soufflé collar to a small 13 cm (5^1/$_2$ in) diameter x 6 cm (2^1/$_2$ in) deep soufflé dish so that the paper stands 6 cm (2^1/$_2$ in) higher than the top of the dish (see page 8).

2 Put the water in a small heatproof bowl or mug and sprinkle over the gelatine, making sure that the water absorbs all the powder. Set aside for 5 minutes, then stand the bowl in a small saucepan half-filled with boiling water and simmer for 3–4 minutes, stirring occasionally, until the gelatine dissolves to a clear liquid.

3 Put the egg yolks and sugar in a large heatproof bowl then stand the bowl over a saucepan of simmering water so that the base of the bowl is not touching the water. Whisk using a hand-held electric whisk for about 10 minutes until the eggs are very thick and pale, and the whisk leaves a trail when lifted above the mixture. Remove the bowl from the heat and continue whisking until cool.

4 Gradually fold in the dissolved gelatine, adding it in a thin, steady stream. Fold in the chestnut purée and brandy, then the melted chocolate. Softly whip the cream (no need to wash the whisk in between), then fold into the soufflé mixture.

5 Wash the whisk and dry it well then use it to whisk the egg whites into stiff, moist-looking peaks. Fold a large spoonful into the soufflé mixture to loosen it then gently fold in the remaining egg whites. Pour the mixture into the prepared soufflé dish so that it stands above the rim of the dish. Chill for 4 hours or until set.

6 To serve, snip the string off the soufflé collar and gently peel away the paper. Top with dark chocolate curls, made by running a swivel vegetable peeler along the smooth underside of a bar of plain dark chocolate. If the curls are very tiny, microwave the bar of chocolate in 15-second bursts until it softens and you can make bigger curls.

healthy soufflés

spicy sweet potato soufflé

1 small sweet potato, about 200 g
   (7 oz), peeled and finely diced

2 tablespoons olive oil, plus extra for
   greasing

2 tablespoons fresh breadcrumbs

25 g (1 oz) butter

1 teaspoon cumin seeds, roughly
   crushed

1 teaspoon fennel seeds, roughly
   crushed

1 garlic clove, crushed

50 g (2 oz) plain flour

300 ml (1/2 pint) skimmed milk

4 eggs, separated

1/2 teaspoon turmeric

1/2 teaspoon paprika

salt and freshly ground black pepper

Serves 4
Preparation time: 30 minutes
Cooking time: 35–40 minutes

The orange colour of this eye-catching soufflé is achieved by mixing sweet potato with vibrant yellow turmeric, deep red paprika, and fennel and cumin seeds crushed using a mortar and pestle to release their full pungency.

1 Cook the diced sweet potato in the top of a steamer for about 5 minutes until just tender. Meanwhile, grease a medium tall 15 cm (6 in) diameter x 9 cm (3 3/4 in) deep soufflé dish with a little olive oil, then line the dish with the breadcrumbs (see page 8). Attach a soufflé collar that stands 7.5 cm (3 in) higher than the top of the dish (see page 8).

2 Melt the butter in a saucepan with the olive oil. Add the crushed seeds and garlic and cook for 1/2 minute. Stir in the flour, then gradually mix in the milk and bring to the boil, stirring until thickened and smooth.

3 Remove the pan from the heat and stir in the egg yolks, turmeric, paprika and some seasoning. Gently stir in the sweet potato and leave to cool.

4 Whisk the egg whites into stiff, moist-looking peaks. Fold a large spoonful into the cooled sauce to loosen the mixture then fold in the remaining egg whites.

5 Pour the mixture into the prepared soufflé dish and bake in a preheated oven, 190°C (375°F), Gas Mark 5, for 25–30 minutes until the soufflé is well risen, the top is browned and there is a slight wobble to the centre.

6 Quickly snip the string off the soufflé collar and gently peel away the paper. Spoon the soufflé on to plates and serve immediately.

minted pea and feta soufflé

2 tablespoons olive oil, plus extra for
    greasing
2 tablespoons ground almonds
25 g (1 oz) butter
50 g (2 oz) plain flour
300 ml (1/2 pint) skimmed milk
4 eggs, separated
75 g (3 oz) feta cheese, drained
    and coarsely grated
125 g (4 oz) frozen peas, defrosted
    and crushed with a fork
3 tablespoons chopped mint
freshly ground black pepper
tomato and onion salad, to serve

Serves 4
Preparation time: 30 minutes
Cooking time: 30–35 minutes

Transform some humble, high-fibre frozen peas into this lightly minted, Greek-inspired soufflé – perfect for a relaxing summer lunch al fresco. Feta cheese has a strong, salty taste, so a little goes a long way and there is no need to add extra salt when seasoning.

1 Grease a medium tall 15 cm (6 in) diameter x 9 cm (3³/4 in) deep soufflé dish with a little olive oil, then line the dish with the ground almonds (see page 8). Attach a soufflé collar that stands 7.5 cm (3 in) higher than the top of the dish (see page 8).

2 Melt the butter in a saucepan with the olive oil. Stir in the flour and cook for 1 minute. Gradually mix in the milk and bring to the boil, stirring until thickened and smooth.

3 Remove the pan from the heat and stir in the egg yolks, crumbled cheese and a little pepper. Leave to cool.

4 Whisk the egg whites into stiff, moist-looking peaks. Stir the peas and mint into the cooled sauce, then fold in a large spoonful of egg whites to loosen the mixture. Gently fold in the remaining egg whites.

5 Pour the mixture into the prepared soufflé dish and bake in a preheated oven, 190°C (375°F), Gas Mark 5, for 25–30 minutes until the soufflé is well risen, the top is browned and there is a slight wobble to the centre.

6 Quickly snip the string off the soufflé collar and gently peel away the paper. Spoon the soufflé on to plates and serve with a tomato and onion salad.

beetroot, ricotta and horseradish soufflés

2 tablespoons olive oil, plus extra for
   greasing
3 tablespoons fresh breadcrumbs
25 g (1 oz) butter
50 g (2 oz) plain flour
300 ml (1/2 pint) skimmed milk
4 eggs, separated
4 teaspoons horseradish sauce
4 tablespoons ricotta cheese
175 g (6 oz) cooked beetroot in their
   own juice, drained and coarsely
   grated
salt and freshly ground black pepper

Serves 4
Preparation time: 30 minutes
Cooking time: 20 minutes

*The amazing purple colour of these soufflés is guaranteed to get your guests
talking, and they make a great reduced-fat dinner party starter.*

1 Grease 4 small 10 cm (4 in) diameter x 6 cm (2¹/2 in) deep soufflé dishes with a
   little olive oil, then line the dishes with the breadcrumbs (see page 8). Stand the
   dishes on a baking sheet.

2 Melt the butter in a saucepan with the olive oil. Stir in the flour and cook for
   1 minute. Gradually mix in the milk and bring to the boil, stirring until thickened
   and smooth.

3 Remove the pan from the heat and stir in the egg yolks and horseradish sauce
   then the ricotta, grated beetroot and some salt and pepper. Leave to cool.

4 Whisk the egg whites into stiff, moist-looking peaks. Fold a large spoonful into the
   cooled sauce to loosen the mixture then gently fold in the remaining egg whites.

5 Spoon the mixture into the prepared soufflé dishes and bake in a preheated oven,
   190°C (375°F), Gas Mark 5, for 15 minutes until the soufflés are well risen, their
   tops are browned and there is a slight wobble to the centres. Serve immediately.

sage, spring onion and raisin soufflés

2 tablespoons olive oil, plus extra for
  greasing
3 tablespoons fresh breadcrumbs
25 g (1 oz) butter
50 g (2 oz) plain flour
300 ml (1/2 pint) skimmed milk
4 eggs, separated
50 g (2 oz) raisins
5 spring onions, thinly sliced
3 tablespoons chopped sage
salt and freshly ground black pepper

Serves 4
Preparation time: 30 minutes
Cooking time: 20 minutes

This is an unusual combination of flavours, but one that works well. To ring the changes, use the same weight of chopped sun-dried tomatoes in oil instead of the raisins or 75–125 g (3–4 oz) of blue cheese, depending on its strength. If you don't have any fresh sage, then mix a little dried sage with some fresh or frozen chopped parsley.

1 Grease 4 small 10 cm (4 in) diameter x 6 cm (2 1/2 in) deep soufflé dishes with a little olive oil, then line the dishes with the breadcrumbs (see page 8). Stand the dishes on a baking sheet.

2 Melt the butter in a saucepan with the olive oil. Stir in the flour and cook for 1 minute. Gradually mix in the milk and bring to the boil, stirring until thickened and smooth.

3 Remove the pan from the heat and stir in the egg yolks, raisins, spring onions, sage and some salt and pepper. Leave to cool.

4 Whisk the egg whites into stiff, moist-looking peaks. Fold a large spoonful into the cooled sauce to loosen the mixture then gently fold in the remaining egg whites.

5 Spoon the mixture into the prepared soufflé dishes and bake in a preheated oven, 190°C (375°F), Gas Mark 5, for 15 minutes until the soufflés are well risen, their tops are browned and there is a slight wobble to the centres. Serve immediately.

hot date and dark chocolate soufflé

butter, for greasing
2 tablespoons ground almonds
125 g (4 oz) pitted dried dates, finely
    chopped
4 tablespoons water
3 egg yolks
2 tablespoons caster sugar
40 g (1 1/2 oz) plain flour
250 ml (8 fl oz) skimmed milk
125 g (4 oz) plain dark chocolate,
    broken into pieces
5 egg whites
sifted icing sugar and cocoa powder,
    for dusting

Serves 4
Preparation time: 30 minutes
Cooking time: 35–40 minutes

This incredibly rich, dark soufflé is irresistible. No one would guess that it's made with dates for natural sweetness and skimmed milk.

1 Lightly butter a medium tall 15 cm (6 in) diameter x 9 cm (3 3/4 in) deep soufflé dish, then line the dish with the ground almonds (see page 8). Attach a soufflé collar that stands 7.5 cm (3 in) higher than the top of the dish (see page 8).

2 Put the dates and the water in a small saucepan, cover and simmer for 5 minutes until soft. Leave to cool.

3 Meanwhile, whisk the egg yolks and caster sugar in a bowl until thick, pale and mousse-like. Sift the flour over the surface, then gently fold it in.

4 Bring the milk just to the boil in a separate saucepan, then gradually whisk it into the egg yolk mixture. Return the milk mixture to the pan and cook over a medium heat, stirring continuously until thickened and smooth. Remove from the heat, add the chocolate and stir until melted. Mix in the dates then leave to cool.

5 Whisk the egg whites into stiff, moist-looking peaks. Fold a large spoonful into the cooled sauce to loosen the mixture then gently fold in the remaining egg whites.

6 Spoon the mixture into the prepared soufflé dish and bake in a preheated oven, 200°C (400°F), Gas Mark 6, for 25–30 minutes until the soufflé is well risen, the top is browned and there is a slight wobble to the centre.

7 Quickly snip the string off the soufflé collar and gently peel away the paper. Dust the top of the soufflé with sifted icing sugar and cocoa powder and serve immediately.

crushed lime, coconut and mango soufflés

4 tablespoons water

4 teaspoons powdered gelatine

4 eggs, separated

50 g (2 oz) caster sugar

3 teaspoons cornflour

400 ml (14 fl oz) can reduced-fat
   coconut milk

1 large mango, peeled, stone removed
   and chopped

grated rind and juice of 2 limes

chopped and halved pistachio nuts,
   to decorate

Serves 6

Preparation time: 30 minutes, plus
   chilling

Cooking time: 10 minutes

Completely dairy free, this chilled soufflé is made with a coconut milk custard, flavoured with lime rind and juice, then mixed with a purée of fresh mango and lightened with whisked egg whites.

1   Attach soufflé collars to 6 individual 7.5 cm (3 in) diameter x 4 cm (1½ in) deep soufflé dishes so that the paper stands 4 cm (1½ in) higher than the top of each dish (see page 8). Stand the dishes on a tray.

2   Put the water in a small heatproof bowl or mug and sprinkle over the gelatine, making sure that the water absorbs all the powder. Set aside for 5 minutes.

3   Whisk the egg yolks, sugar and cornflour in a bowl until thick and pale. Bring the coconut milk just to the boil in a saucepan then gradually whisk it into the egg yolk mixture. Return the milk mixture to the pan.

4   Cook the coconut custard over a medium heat, stirring continuously until it is thickened and smooth and the custard coats the back of the wooden spoon. Remove from the heat, add the soaked gelatine and stir until it has completely dissolved. Leave to cool.

5   Blend the chopped mango in a liquidizer or food processor until smooth. Stir into the coconut custard with the lime rind and juice and chill in the refrigerator until it is just beginning to set. (If the custard seems to be taking a long time to thicken in the refrigerator, transfer it to the freezer for 10–15 minutes.)

6   Whisk the egg whites into stiff, moist-looking peaks. Fold a large spoonful into the setting coconut custard to loosen the mixture then gently fold in the remaining egg whites. Pour the mixture into the prepared soufflé dishes so that it stands above the rim of the dishes. Chill for 4 hours or until set.

7   To serve, snip the string off the soufflé collars and gently peel away the paper. Press the chopped pistachio nuts around the sides of the soufflés with a knife and arrange a few nut halves on top, to decorate.

warm vanilla and prune soufflés

butter, for greasing
3 tablespoons ground almonds
1 vanilla pod
250 ml (8 fl oz) skimmed milk
3 egg yolks
50 g (2 oz) caster sugar
40 g (1 1/2 oz) plain flour
5 egg whites
150 g (5 oz) ready-to-eat pitted prunes,
    finely chopped
sifted icing sugar, for dusting

Serves 4
Preparation time: 30 minutes
Cooking time: 15–20 minutes

Well known for being rich in fibre, prunes are also naturally sweet so that the amount of sugar in this soufflé is less than usual. While this doesn't affect the finished flavour, it helps to reduce the calories greatly in this very moreish dessert.

1 Lightly butter 4 small 10 cm (4 in) diameter x 6 cm (2 1/2 in) deep soufflé dishes, then line the dishes with the ground almonds (see page 8). Stand the dishes on a baking sheet.

2 Cut a slit along the length of the vanilla pod, then place it in a saucepan with the milk and bring just to the boil. Set aside for 15 minutes for the vanilla flavour to develop.

3 Whisk the egg yolks and caster sugar in a bowl until thick, pale and mousse-like. Sift the flour over the surface, then gently fold it in.

4 Lift the vanilla pod out of the milk, scrape the black seeds from the inside of the pod and add to the milk. Reheat the milk, then gradually whisk it into the egg yolk mixture. Return the milk mixture to the pan and heat, stirring continuously until thickened and smooth. Leave to cool.

5 Whisk the egg whites into stiff, moist-looking peaks. Stir the chopped prunes into the cooled sauce, then fold in a large spoonful of egg whites to loosen the mixture. Gently fold in the remaining egg whites.

6 Spoon the mixture into the prepared soufflé dishes and bake in a preheated oven, 220°C (425°F), Gas Mark 7, for 10–12 minutes until the soufflés are well risen, their tops are browned and there is a slight wobble to the centres. Dust the tops of the soufflés liberally with sifted icing sugar and serve immediately.

saffron and smooth apricot soufflé

175 g (6 oz) ready-to-eat dried apricots
1/4 teaspoon saffron threads
150 ml (1/4 pint) water, plus
   4 tablespoons
4 teaspoons powdered gelatine
4 eggs, separated
50 g (2 oz) caster sugar
250 g (8 oz) fromage frais

Serves 6
Preparation time: 30 minutes, plus
   chilling
Cooking time: 23–24 minutes

This pretty, pale orange-coloured chilled soufflé combines the flavour of apricots with a subtle hint of saffron. Although virtually fat-free fromage frais is used here in place of double cream, it is hard to taste the difference.

1 Attach a soufflé collar to a small 13 cm (5 1/2 in) diameter x 6 cm (2 1/2 in) deep soufflé dish so that the paper stands 6 cm (2 1/2 in) higher than the top of the dish (see page 8).

2 Put the apricots, saffron and the 150 ml (1/4 pint) of water in a small saucepan, cover and simmer for 10 minutes until softened. Blend in a liquidizer or food processor until smooth and leave to cool.

3 Put the remaining water in a small heatproof bowl or mug and sprinkle over the gelatine, making sure that the water absorbs all the powder. Set aside for 5 minutes, then stand the bowl in a small saucepan half-filled with boiling water and simmer for 3–4 minutes, stirring occasionally, until the gelatine dissolves to a clear liquid.

4 Put the egg yolks and sugar in a large heatproof bowl then stand the bowl over a saucepan of simmering water so that the base of the bowl is not touching the water. Whisk using a hand-held electric whisk for about 10 minutes until the eggs are very thick and pale, and the whisk leaves a trail when lifted above the mixture. Remove the bowl from the heat and continue whisking until cool.

5 Gradually fold in the dissolved gelatine, adding it in a thin, steady stream, then fold in the apricot purée and the fromage frais. Chill until just beginning to set.

6 Whisk the egg whites into stiff, moist-looking peaks. Fold a large spoonful into the apricot mixture to loosen it then gently fold in the remaining egg whites. Pour the mixture into the prepared soufflé dish so that it stands above the rim of the dish. Chill for 4 hours or until set. To serve, snip the string off the soufflé collar and gently peel away the paper.

honeyed banana soufflés with fresh figs

4 tablespoons water
4 teaspoons powdered gelatine
4 eggs, separated
3 tablespoons thick-set flower honey
2 bananas, about 400 g (13 oz) in total,
   weighed with skins on
2 tablespoons freshly squeezed lemon
   juice
250 g (8 oz) low-fat Greek yogurt

To decorate
50 g (2 oz) flaked almonds, toasted and
   roughly chopped (optional)
1 fresh fig, cut into 6 wedges

Serves 6
Preparation time: 30 minutes, plus
   chilling
Cooking time: 13–14 minutes

Thick-set flower honey is used here for its superior flavour and mixed with low-fat Greek yogurt and naturally sweet ripe bananas for a delicate, fresh-tasting chilled soufflé. The soufflé tops have been decorated with wedges of fresh fig, but slices of banana dipped in lemon juice or a few fresh raspberries could be used instead.

1   Attach soufflé collars to 6 individual 7.5 cm (3 in) diameter x 4 cm (1 1/2 in) deep soufflé dishes so that the paper stands 4 cm (1 1/2 in) higher than the top of each dish (see page 8).

2   Put the water in a small heatproof bowl or mug and sprinkle over the gelatine, making sure that the water absorbs all the powder. Set aside for 5 minutes, then stand the bowl in a small saucepan half-filled with boiling water and simmer for 3–4 minutes, stirring occasionally, until the gelatine dissolves to a clear liquid.

3   Put the egg yolks and honey in a large heatproof bowl, then stand the bowl over a saucepan of simmering water so that the base of the bowl is not touching the water. Whisk using a hand-held electric whisk for about 10 minutes until the eggs are very thick and pale, and the whisk leaves a trail when lifted above the mixture. Remove the bowl from the heat and continue whisking until cool.

4   Gradually fold in the dissolved gelatine, adding it in a thin, steady stream. Mash the bananas on a plate with the lemon juice, then fold into the egg yolk mixture with the yogurt.

5   Whisk the egg whites into stiff, moist-looking peaks. Fold a large spoonful into the mixture to loosen it then gently fold in the remaining egg whites. Spoon the mixture into the prepared soufflé dishes so that it stands above the rim of the dishes. Chill for 4 hours or until set.

6   To serve, snip the string off the soufflé collars and gently peel away the paper. Press the toasted almonds, if using, around the sides of the soufflés with a knife and arrange the fig wedges on top, to decorate.

soufflés with
a difference

mushroom and pancetta soufflé omelette

1 tablespoon olive oil
175 g (6 oz) mixed wild or cup
    mushrooms, sliced
125 g (4 oz) pancetta or gammon
    steak, diced
3 tablespoons full-fat crème fraîche
4 teaspoons chopped thyme
4 eggs, separated
1/2 teaspoon Dijon mustard
20 g (3/4 oz) butter
salt and freshly ground black pepper
mixed salad, to serve

Serves 2
Preparation time: 15 minutes
Cooking time: 10–12 minutes

This recipe transforms simple eggs and bacon into a supper dish that is more sophisticated, but doesn't take much longer to make. Unlike other omelettes, a soufflé omelette does not require stirring during cooking.

1 Heat the oil in a large frying pan, add the mushrooms and pancetta or ham, and fry for 5 minutes, stirring frequently, until golden. Stir in the crème fraîche and thyme, then slide the mixture out of the pan and keep hot.

2 Wash and dry the pan. Whisk the egg whites into stiff, moist-looking peaks. Mix together the egg yolks, mustard and some salt and pepper, then fold into the egg whites.

3 Heat the butter in the frying pan, add the egg mixture and cook over a medium heat for 3–4 minutes until the underside is golden. Quickly transfer the pan to a hot grill and cook for 2–3 minutes until the top is brown and the centre still slightly soft, making sure that the handle is away from the heat.

4 Spoon the mushroom and pancetta mixture over the omelette and fold in half. Serve immediately with a mixed salad.

sweet soufflé omelette with strawberries

375 g (12 oz) strawberries, hulled and
   thickly sliced, plus extra to decorate
2 tablespoons redcurrant jelly
2 teaspoons balsamic vinegar
5 eggs, separated
4 tablespoons icing sugar, sifted
25 g (1 oz) butter

Serves 4
Preparation time: 15 minutes
Cooking time: 8–10 minutes

*Balsamic vinegar is a surprising addition to this recipe, but its slight sharpness
helps to reduce the richness of the light, fluffy, cloud-like sweet omelette.
Make and serve this omelette at the very last minute for maximum volume.*

1 Warm the sliced strawberries, redcurrant jelly and vinegar together in a
saucepan until the jelly has just melted.

2 Meanwhile, whisk the egg whites into stiff, moist-looking peaks. Mix the
egg yolks with 1 tablespoon of the sugar, then fold into the egg whites.

3 Heat the butter in a large frying pan, add the egg mixture and cook over a
medium heat for 3–4 minutes until the underside is golden. Quickly transfer
the pan to a hot grill and cook for 2–3 minutes until the top is browned and the
centre still slightly soft, making sure that the handle is away from the heat.

4 Spoon the warm strawberry mixture over the omelette, fold in half and dust
with the remaining sugar. Cut into 4 and serve with extra strawberries.

iced strawberry daiquiri soufflé

This gelatine-free soufflé is made with a base of Italian meringue, a stiff meringue that is mixed with a hot sugar syrup rather than oven baked, and flavoured with whipped double cream and the traditional daiquiri ingredients of lime and white rum.

500 g (1 lb) fresh strawberries, hulled,
    plus extra halved to decorate
200 g (7 oz) caster sugar
1 tablespoon liquid glucose
3 tablespoons water
4 eggs, separated
250 ml (8 fl oz) double cream
finely grated rind and juice of 2 limes
4 tablespoons white rum

Serves 6–8
Preparation time: 40 minutes, plus
    freezing
Cooking time: 10 minutes

1 Attach a soufflé collar to a medium 16.5 cm (6¾ in) diameter x 7.5 cm (3 in) deep soufflé dish so that the paper stands 7.5 cm (3 in) higher than the top of the dish (see page 8).

2 Blend the strawberries in a liquidizer or food processor until smooth, then press through a sieve.

3 Gently heat the sugar, liquid glucose and water in a small saucepan, without stirring, until the sugar has completely dissolved. Add a sugar thermometer and heat to 110°C (230°F), still without stirring.

4 Meanwhile, put the egg whites in a large bowl. When the sugar thermometer reaches the required temperature, begin whisking the egg whites and continue heating the sugar syrup to 121°C (250°F).

5 Once the temperature is reached, begin to pour the boiling syrup slowly into the egg whites as you whisk. Continue whisking for 10–15 minutes until the meringue mixture has cooled.

6 Softly whip the cream, then add the lime rind and gradually whisk in the juice and rum. Fold in the strawberry purée.

7 Fold the strawberry mixture into the meringue mixture, one-third at a time, until completely mixed. Pour the mixture into the prepared soufflé dish so that it stands above the rim of the dish. Freeze overnight until firm.

8 To serve, snip the string off the soufflé collar and gently peel away the paper. Decorate the top with the extra strawberries. Scoop immediately from the dish using a warmed spoon.

gingered chocolate roulade

5 eggs, separated
175 g (6 oz) caster sugar, plus extra for
    sprinkling
200 g (7 oz) plain dark chocolate,
    melted
2 tablespoons warm water

Filling
250 ml (8 fl oz) double cream
2 tablespoons chopped glacé ginger

To decorate
chocolate curls (see method)
sifted icing sugar, for dusting

Serves 6–8
Preparation time: 40 minutes, plus
    cooling
Cooking time: 15–20 minutes

This popular Christmas dessert can be made and frozen in advance. For a summer version, add fresh raspberries or strawberries in place of the ginger. The absence of flour makes this especially good for people on a wheat-free diet.

1 Line a 23 x 30 cm (9 x 12 in) roasting tin with baking parchment and snip into the corners so that the paper fits snugly.

2 Whisk the egg yolks and caster sugar in a large bowl until thick and pale, and the whisk leaves a trail when lifted above the mixture. Add the melted chocolate and warm water and gently fold together.

3 Wash the whisk and dry it well then use it to whisk the egg whites into stiff, moist-looking peaks. Fold a large spoonful into the chocolate mixture to loosen it then gently fold in the remaining egg whites.

4 Spoon the mixture into the prepared tin and ease it into the corners. Bake the roulade in a preheated oven, 180°C (350°F), Gas Mark 4, for 15–20 minutes until it is well risen and the top feels crusty to the touch. Cover with a clean tea towel and leave to cool for at least 4 hours.

5 Meanwhile, make the decorative chocolate curls. Run a swivel-bladed vegetable peeler along the smooth underside of a bar of plain dark chocolate. If the curls are very tiny, microwave the bar of chocolate in 15-second bursts until it softens and you can make bigger curls. Set aside.

6 Softly whip the cream, then fold in the glacé ginger. Wet a clean tea towel, wring out and place on the work surface so that a short edge is nearest you. Cover with a large piece of baking parchment and sprinkle with a little caster sugar. Turn the cooled roulade out on to the paper, remove the tin and peel away the lining paper. Spread the roulade with the gingered cream, then roll it up, starting from the shortest side nearest you, using the sugared paper and tea towel to help.

7 Transfer the roulade to a serving plate, top with chocolate curls and dust with icing sugar. Cut into thick slices to serve.

hazelnut and pear roulade with mascarpone

125 g (4 oz) hazelnuts

5 eggs, separated

175 g (6 oz) caster sugar, plus extra for sprinkling

1 just-ripe pear, peeled and coarsely grated

Filling

200 g (7 oz) mascarpone cheese

2 tablespoons icing sugar

250 g (8 oz) fresh apricots, stoned and roughly chopped

Serves 6–8

Preparation time: 30 minutes, plus cooling

Cooking time: 18–19 minutes

Toasted hazelnuts, juicy pears and creamy smooth mascarpone encased in a light-as-air sponge make this an irresistible cake for a special afternoon tea. When fresh apricots are out of season, use a well-drained 411 g (13 1/2 oz) can of apricot halves instead.

1 Line a 23 x 30 cm (9 x 12 in) roasting tin with baking parchment and snip into the corners so that the paper fits snugly.

2 Put the hazelnuts on a piece of foil and toast under the grill for 3–4 minutes until golden. Roughly chop 2 tablespoons and set aside for decoration, then grind the remainder in a liquidizer or food processor until very finely chopped.

3 Whisk the egg yolks and caster sugar in a large bowl until thick and pale, and the whisk leaves a trail when lifted above the mixture. Fold the toasted finely chopped hazelnuts and grated pear into the egg yolk mixture.

4 Wash the whisk and dry it well then use it to whisk the egg whites into stiff, moist-looking peaks. Fold a large spoonful into the nut mixture to loosen it, then gently fold in the remaining egg whites.

5 Spoon the mixture into the prepared tin and ease it into the corners. Bake the roulade in a preheated oven, 180°C (350°F), Gas Mark 4, for 15 minutes until it is well risen, golden brown and the top feels spongy. Cover with a clean tea towel and leave to cool for at least 1 hour.

6 Beat the mascarpone cheese and icing sugar together until soft. Wet a clean tea towel, wring out and place on the work surface so that a short edge is nearest you. Cover with a large piece of baking parchment and sprinkle with a little caster sugar. Turn the cooled roulade out on to the paper, remove the tin and peel away the lining paper.

7 Spread the roulade with the mascarpone mixture, then sprinkle with the apricots. Roll up the roulade, starting from the shortest side nearest you, using the sugared paper and tea towel to help. Transfer the roulade to a serving plate, sprinkle over the roughly chopped hazelnuts and cut into thick slices to serve.

watercress and salmon roulade

40 g (1¹/2 oz) butter
40 g (1¹/2 oz) plain flour
250 ml (8 fl oz) milk
4 eggs, separated
75 g (3 oz) watercress, roughly chopped,
    plus a few extra leaves to garnish
grated rind of 1 lime
3 tablespoons ready-grated Parmesan
    cheese
salt and freshly ground black pepper
lime wedges, to garnish

Filling
300 g (10 oz) salmon fillet, halved
200 ml (7 fl oz) full-fat crème fraîche
2 tablespoons freshly squeezed lime
    juice
salt and freshly ground black pepper

Serves 4–6
Preparation time: 30 minutes, plus
    cooling
Cooking time: 23–30 minutes

This roulade would be ideal served at a summer wedding anniversary or christening party. If serving it as part of a large buffet, cut it into 10 slices and make two, three or more the day before required. Refrigerating the finished roulade, tightly wrapped in paper, for at least 30 minutes makes slicing easier.

1 Line a 23 x 30 cm (9 x 12 in) roasting tin with baking parchment and snip into the corners so that the paper fits snugly.

2 Melt the butter in a saucepan, stir in the flour and cook for 1 minute. Gradually mix in the milk and bring to the boil, stirring until thickened and smooth. Remove from the heat and stir in the egg yolks, watercress, lime rind and salt and pepper. Leave to cool for 15 minutes.

3 Whisk the egg whites into stiff, moist-looking peaks. Fold a large spoonful into the cooled sauce to loosen the mixture then fold in the remaining egg whites. Spoon the mixture into the prepared tin and ease into the corners.

4 Bake the roulade in a preheated oven, 180°C (350°F), Gas Mark 4, for 15–20 minutes until it is well risen, golden brown and the top feels spongy. Cover with a clean tea towel and leave to cool for at least 1 hour.

5 Meanwhile, steam the salmon for 8–10 minutes until it just flakes and the flakes are the same opaque colour all the way through. Leave to cool, before skinning, flaking and discarding any bones. Beat the crème fraîche with the lime juice and plenty of salt and pepper.

6 Wet a clean tea towel, wring out and place on the work surface so that a short edge is nearest you. Cover with a large piece of baking parchment and sprinkle with the Parmesan. Turn the cooled roulade out on to the paper, remove the tin and peel away the lining paper.

7 Spread the roulade with the crème fraîche mixture, then the salmon. Roll up the roulade, starting from the shortest side nearest you, using the paper and tea towel to help. Cut into thick slices and serve garnished with a few watercress leaves and lime wedges.

spinach and prosciutto roulade

300 g (10 oz) frozen leaf spinach,
  defrosted
40 g (1½ oz) butter
40 g (1½ oz) plain flour
250 ml (8 fl oz) milk
4 eggs, separated
large pinch of grated nutmeg
3 tablespoons ready-grated Parmesan
  cheese
salt and freshly ground black pepper
roasted pepper and tomato salad,
  to serve (optional)

Filling
200 g (7 oz) cream cheese with garlic
  and herbs, stirred to soften
6 slices of prosciutto

Serves 4–6
Preparation time: 30 minutes, plus
  cooling
Cooking time: 15–20 minutes

If you have time, roll up the filled roulade an hour or so before you need it, then keep it wrapped in nonstick baking paper to set the shape and make slicing easier. For vegetarians, substitute thin slices of bottled red pimiento for the prosciutto.

1 Line a 23 x 30 cm (9 x 12 in) roasting tin with baking parchment and snip into the corners so that the paper fits snugly. Put the spinach in a sieve set over a bowl and press out any water using the back of a spoon.

2 Melt the butter in a saucepan, stir in the flour and cook for 1 minute. Gradually mix in the milk and bring to the boil, stirring until thickened and smooth. Remove the pan from the heat and stir in the spinach, egg yolks, nutmeg and some salt and pepper. Leave to cool for 15 minutes.

3 Whisk the egg whites into stiff, moist-looking peaks. Fold a large spoonful into the cooled sauce to loosen the mixture then gently fold in the remaining egg whites. Spoon the mixture into the prepared tin and ease into the corners.

4 Bake the roulade in a preheated oven, 180°C (350°F), Gas Mark 4, for 15–20 minutes until it is well risen, golden brown and the top feels spongy. Cover with a clean tea towel and leave to cool for at least 1 hour.

5 Wet a clean tea towel, wring out and place on the work surface so that a short edge is nearest you. Cover with a large piece of baking parchment and sprinkle with the Parmesan. Turn the cooled roulade out on to the paper, remove the tin and peel away the lining paper.

6 Spread the roulade with the cream cheese and cover with slices of prosciutto. Roll up the roulade, starting from the shortest side nearest you, using the paper and tea towel to help. Cut into thick slices and serve 1 slice per person for a starter or 2 for a light supper with a roasted pepper and tomato salad.

prawn, gruyère and leek roulade

40 g (1½ oz) butter
40 g (1½ oz) plain flour
250 ml (8 fl oz) milk
4 eggs, separated
75 g (3 oz) Gruyère cheese, grated
1 teaspoon Dijon mustard
300 g (10 oz) small frozen cooked
   peeled prawns prawns, just
   defrosted, rinsed and well drained
2 tablespoons ready-grated Parmesan
   cheese

Filling
25 g (1 oz) butter
1 tablespoon olive oil
400 g (13 oz) leeks, slit, well rinsed and
   very thinly sliced
salt and freshly ground black pepper

Serves 4–6
Preparation time: 30 minutes
Cooking time: 19–25 minutes

This very moreish cheesy roulade dotted with prawns is filled with a green ribbon of sautéed leeks. Serve with new potatoes for a supper dish or as a sophisticated dinner party dish served in a pool of warmed canned lobster bisque.

1 Line a 23 x 30 cm (9 x 12 in) roasting tin with baking parchment and snip into the corners so that the paper fits snugly.

2 Melt the butter in a saucepan, stir in the flour and cook for 1 minute. Gradually mix in the milk and bring to the boil, stirring until thickened and smooth. Remove from the heat and stir in the egg yolks, cheese, mustard and the roulade. Leave to cool for 15 minutes.

3 Whisk the egg whites into stiff, moist-looking peaks. Fold the prawns into the cooled sauce, then a large spoonful of egg whites to loosen the mixture. Gently fold in the remaining egg whites. Spoon the mixture into the prepared tin and ease into the corners.

4 Bake the roulade in a preheated oven, 180°C (350°F), Gas Mark 4, for 15–20 minutes until it is well risen, golden brown and the top feels spongy. Meanwhile, make the leek filling. Heat the butter and oil in a frying pan, add the leeks and sauté for 4–5 minutes, stirring frequently, until softened. Season with some salt and pepper.

5 Wet a clean tea towel, wring out and place on the work surface so that a short edge is nearest you. Cover with a large piece of baking parchment and sprinkle with the Parmesan. Turn the hot roulade out on to the paper, remove the tin and peel away the lining paper. Cover the roulade with the hot leeks and roll up, starting from the shortest side nearest you, using the paper and tea towel to help.

6 Cut the roulade into thick slices and serve 1 slice per person for a starter or 2 for a light supper.

cheese and sun-blushed tomato soufflé tart

20 g (3/4 oz) butter, plus extra for
 greasing
375 g (12 oz) shortcrust pastry,
 defrosted if frozen
20 g (3/4 oz) plain flour
150 ml (1/4 pint) milk
3 eggs, separated
2 teaspoons chopped rosemary
100 g (31/2 oz) individual goats' cheese,
 diced
2 teaspoons Dijon mustard
7 g (31/2 oz) sun-blushed tomatoes in
 oil, drained and sliced
salt and freshly ground black pepper

Serves 6
Preparation time: 40 minutes, plus
 chilling
Cooking time: 45–50 minutes

*Rather than simply forking together eggs and milk for a tart filling, here the eggs
have been separated and whisked for extra volume and lightness, then flavoured
with goats' cheese and rosemary and baked over a layer of sun-blushed tomatoes.*

1 Lightly butter a 23 cm (9 in) deep loose-bottomed tart tin. Roll the pastry out
 thinly on a lightly floured surface until a little larger than the tin, then lift over a
 rolling pin into the tin. Press into the base and sides, trim off the excess pastry
 and prick the base with a fork. Chill for 15 minutes.

2 Line the tart case with a piece of greaseproof or baking parchment and baking
 beans. Set on a baking sheet and bake in a preheated oven, 190°C (375°F),
 Gas Mark 5, for 10 minutes. Remove the paper and beans and cook for 5 more
 minutes until golden brown around the edges.

3 Meanwhile, melt the butter in a saucepan, stir in the flour and cook for
 1 minute. Gradually mix in the milk and bring to the boil, stirring until thickened
 and smooth. Remove from the heat and stir in the egg yolks, rosemary, goats'
 cheese and some salt and pepper. Leave to cool for 15 minutes.

4 Spread the base of the pastry case with the mustard and cover with the sliced
 sun-blushed tomatoes.

5 Whisk the egg whites into stiff, moist-looking peaks. Fold a large spoonful into
 the cooled sauce to loosen the mixture then gently fold in the remaining egg
 whites. Spoon the mixture into the tart case and bake for 25–30 minutes until
 golden brown and just set. Serve warm, cut into wedges.

double chocolate soufflé tart

Pastry
200 g (7 oz) plain flour
2 tablespoons cocoa powder
50 g (2 oz) caster sugar
125 g (4 oz) butter, diced, plus extra
    for greasing
2¹/₂–3 tablespoons water

Filling
125 g (4 oz) white chocolate, broken
    into pieces
25 g (1 oz) butter
4 eggs, separated
75 g (3 oz) caster sugar
grated rind of 1/2 orange
75 g (3 oz) plain dark chocolate,
    chopped

To decorate
icing sugar, for dusting
white chocolate curls (see page 61)
orange rind curls (see page 57)

orange segments, to serve

Serves 6
Preparation time: 40 minutes, plus
    chilling
Cooking time: 35 minutes

This is perhaps not a true soufflé, but one that combines all the traditional elements of whisked yolks and sugar gently folded with light-as-air whisked whites, flavoured with melted white chocolate and encased in a rich, dark, buttery chocolate pastry.

1 To make the tart case, put the flour, cocoa powder, caster sugar and butter in a bowl and rub in the butter until the mixture resembles fine crumbs. Stir in enough of the water to make a smooth, soft dough. Knead lightly then roll out on a lightly floured surface and use to line a 23 cm (9 in) buttered, loose-bottomed tart tin. Trim off the excess pastry, prick the base with a fork and chill for 15 minutes.

2 Line the tart case with greaseproof or baking parchment and baking beans. Set on a baking sheet and bake in a preheated oven, 190°C (375°F), Gas Mark 5, for 10 minutes. Remove the paper and beans and cook for 5 more minutes.

3 Reduce the oven temperature to 180°C (350°F), Gas Mark 4. Melt the white chocolate and butter in a large heatproof bowl set over a saucepan of just-boiled water.

4 Make the filling by whisking the egg yolks, caster sugar and orange rind in a large bowl until thick and pale, and the whisk leaves a trail when lifted above the mixture. Fold in the melted chocolate and butter.

5 Wash the whisk and dry it well then use it to whisk the egg whites into stiff, moist-looking peaks. Fold a large spoonful into the white chocolate mixture to loosen it then fold in the remaining egg whites.

6 Sprinkle the dark chocolate on to the base of the tart case, then cover with the white chocolate mixture. Bake for 20 minutes until the filling is well risen, the top feels crusty and there is a slight wobble to the centre. Check after 15 minutes and cover lightly with foil if the filling seems to be browning too quickly. Leave to cool – as the tart cools, the filling will sink slightly.

7 Remove the tart from the tin and place on a serving plate. Dust with icing sugar and top with white chocolate curls. Serve cut into wedges with some orange segments.

index

acknowledgements

Photography Lis Parsons
Food Styling Sara Lewis